Helgemo's World of Bridge

The Maestro reveals his secrets

Geo Tislevoll
with Geir Helgemo

FIVE
ACES

First published in Great Britain in 2000
by Five Aces Books
73 Totteridge Lane, High Wycombe, Bucks HP13 7QA, England

© Geo Tislevoll

British Library Cataloguing in Publication Data.
A CIP record of this book is available on request from the British Library.

ISBN 0-9536752-5-4

Typeset by
Wakewing, 73 Totteridge Lane, High Wycombe, Bucks HP13 7QA

Printed in Great Britain by
The Cromwell Press, Trowbridge

Contents

Preface

Helgemo's World of Bridge contains hands and stories from Geir Helgemo's amazing career – so far. The most extraordinary fact about this book may be that when the original Norwegian version of this book was finished, Geir was not yet thirty years old. Despite his youth, Helgemo has achieved an astonishing success at bridge.

The title is a pointer to the sort of nomadic life Geir has led as a globetrotter, playing in all kinds of championships, all over the world. The title also has another meaning. The book is my own attempt to delve into the champion's inner world, to read his mind, so to speak. Why does he think like he does, what are his strengths, and what makes his bridge so special? Is it possible to borrow some of his tricks of the trade?

Helgemo's World of Bridge contains six sections. In them we move between different stages of his career, without following any chronological sequence. In addition, the sections are split up into chapters, which contain one or more hands.

Helgemo himself has contributed a lot to this book. However, I have provided the commentary; any praise for, or jokes about, Geir are my doing. Helgemo has told me most of the stories, and he has also contributed significantly to the bridge analyses.

The book was originally written when Geir had a short break from international bridge. He sat out from the Norwegian team for a couple of international events in 1999 and had a chance to reflect on his career thus far. There were many people hoping he soon would be playing for Norway again. And in January 2000 he was back, playing for the Norwegian team that nearly reached the final of the Bermuda Bowl, which as it happened was held in Bermuda.

Geo Tislevoll
June 2000

Foreword

Geir Helgemo is a bridge phenomenon. Although 'junior' in bridge terms means under 25 years old, it is relatively rare for players to go from their national junior team into the open category. Generally speaking, it takes a few more years of maturity to reach that stage. I would say that most players peak in their late thirties or early forties, while many players at international level are in their sixties and seventies.

Geir first played in the Norwegian Under 25 team when he was 18, and his debut in their open team was when he was 21. Before he was 30 years old (his thirtieth birthday is in the year 2000), he had been established as his country's top player for several years. And that is not just 'any' European country. In the 1990s, Norway has won a bronze and a silver medal in the Bermuda Bowl, as well as several medals in European teams championships.

As well as being one of the world's top players, he is one of the most popular and always has a smile and a nice word for all around him. This book, which was first published in Norwegian, is the first to appear about the 'whizz kid of bridge', but the one thing I am sure of is that it won't be the last. We will be reading of his successes and trying to emulate his thought processes for many years to come.

Omar Sharif
June 2000

Acknowledgements

I would like to thank many people for helping me with this book, and for giving me inspiration to go for the project. First of all, I must thank the 'star' – Geir Helgemo – the man responsible for all the good bridge I am able to write about. He has also contributed a lot of work with the analysis, and by telling me most of the stories.

In addition, I would like to thank Petter Osbak and Einar Asbjørn Brenne, both good friends of Geir and myself, for their help with the proof-reading.

Without the help of Barry Rigal, 'the Englishman in New York', I would not have been able to make the book readable. My English is not very good and I was quite anxious about the result after I had translated it from the Norwegian, especially the humorous parts which could sound quite silly if not translated properly. Barry managed to understand my 'Scandinavian-English', and make sense of it all.

Mor-Åse, Helgemos mother, was a great help. She is naturally a big fan of her son, and provided me with endless clips from magazines and newspaper columns.

Several people were helpful in providing photographs, thanks to Boye Brogeland, Chris Cooper, Mark Horton, Jeff Rubens, Tommy Sandsmark and Jan van Cleeff.

Finally, my gratitude to Geir's opponents through his short career to date. They have tried to halt his progress, but haven't been able to. If he continues with his meteoric rise, maybe there will be a follow-up book in a few years' time.

Introduction

The lady and the boy...

1982. We were in the middle of an ice-cold winter. There were snowy roads everywhere, but nothing could stop us. Three of my bridge friends and I set out early in the morning to go to Glåmos, a mountain village two hours' drive from Trondheim in mid-Norway.

Of course the reason for the trip was to go to a bridge tournament. We tested the nightlife in Røros – the nearest town – the evening before the bridge tournament. But we still felt pretty sharp when the event started. However, the tournament was not really a major event from our perspective. I cannot even remember much about the results. The only difference from the hundreds of tournaments I participated in both before and after this one was what happened in one of the last rounds.

We sat down to play against an old lady, probably almost eighty years old. That was not so unusual, but her partner was a young boy! His head only just came over the top of the table. We could see he was having a really good time. 'This is my first bridge tournament', the proud kid told us. Of course we took a liking to him. He could not have been more than twelve years old – not even a teenager! Somebody recognised a newsworthy story in this and took pictures of the kid and the lady playing against some of the more established players from Trondheim. His smile must have stretched from one ear to the other. He looked like he was thinking: 'Maybe one day I can beat these guys from town?' His dream was going to come true.

Norway has always had good junior players. But ten years after we met the boy and the lady in Glåmos, bridge players all over the country understood that a very special junior had arrived on the scene. Geir Helgemo had moved from his hometown, Røros, to Trondheim to study at the university – at least that was what most people believed. The truth was that he was in Trondheim to play bridge. And we could easily tell he was one of a kind.

One day, a few bridge friends were talking about at what age we had started our bridge careers. Geir asked me: 'Do you remember the day they took that picture of us in Glåmos?'

To be honest I had never realised that it was him.

'Well, I remember the incident. Yes, of course, it was you.'

'So you remember it,' Geir continued, 'but do you recall what happened when you met us?' With a smile I had to admit the data was wiped from my files. 'You bid a grand slam in no-trumps,' he said.

'Oh, yes? Did we make it?'

'My lead gave your partner the thirteenth trick. You could actually make Seven Hearts on your cards, but you played in no-trumps.'

'How old were you when this happened?' I asked.

'Twelve. I had learned bridge the very same month.'

'But you can remember it … hmm … tell me, what happened?'

Geir looked as if he was going to tell me some kind of disaster from a big final, but soon he smiled again.

'Tell me. Come on.'

'OK, but it was ridiculous. Your partner had bid his diamonds and you had shown spades and hearts. Then you landed in Seven No-Trumps and I was on lead with this hand:

♠ 9 8 2
♡ 8 7 2
◇ Q J 2
♣ 8 6 3 2

'What was your choice? Spades, maybe?'

Geir got a funny look in his face.

'No. You see, I was a real beginner. One of the few things I had learned so far was to lead from strength. Attitude, you know. So the two of diamonds seemed a logical opening shot. And this was the full deal:

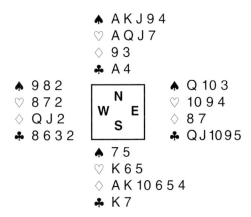

                ♠ A K J 9 4
                ♡ A Q J 7
                ◇ 9 3
                ♣ A 4
    ♠ 9 8 2   ♠ Q 10 3
    ♡ 8 7 2   N   ♡ 10 9 4
    ◇ Q J 2   W   E   ◇ 8 7
    ♣ 8 6 3 2   S   ♣ Q J 10 9 5
                ♠ 7 5
                ♡ K 6 5
                ◇ A K 10 6 5 4
                ♣ K 7

After having written down all the cards, from a hand which gave him a complete bottom in his first tournament, he said with a laugh: 'My spectacular lead of the two of diamonds was not a success. South took trick one with his ten. He then cashed the ace and claimed when he realised the suit was splitting 3-2.'

So, we had bid and made a terrible grand slam, but I could not recall it! The reason I could not was, of course, that my partner had claimed at trick two. I wrongly believed his diamonds were solid, an error which I presumably also made during the bidding. And the guy who told me about it, ten years after it happened, admitted having made a 'loco-lead'. But he had been a beginner, and only twelve years old. Such things happen from time to time. Still, he

remembered everything that had occurred – in detail! This told me something, but I could not understand what. Some years later I understood.

The full story about our play against the lady and the boy was told to me in 1991, the same year the 21-year-old Geir Helgemo made his debut for Norway in the Open European Championship. His performance so far, up to the year 2000, has made it possible to do something as unusual as to write a bridge book about a player not yet thirty years old. Many people believed he would become a great player. But his achievements so far are way beyond all predictions.

Playing for Norway, he has usually partnered Tor Helness, in most people's view the second best player in Norway, and the only one to get anywhere near Geir's level. But not many – especially outside Norway – know that Geir has not partnered Tor much in national tournaments. He has partnered quite a few players and achieved top results with them all.

But not long after his first successes, internationally sponsored teams showed interest in the young Norwegian. For many years now he has been a member of Rita Shugart's team. Rita lives in California, but has lately had Europeans on her team when playing the US Nationals. Geir's partner on these occasions is Tony Forrester from England, and the team is made up with Andrew Robson, also from England, partnering Rita.

A summary of all the top results Geir has achieved would be a long list. Before I start telling bridge stories I'll mention some of the titles and results.

Results in Norway

- Norwegian champion, junior
- Norwegian champion, pairs
- Norwegian champion, teams
- Norwegian champion, mixed pairs
- Winner of the Premier League of Norway

He was won many of these titles several times. In other words, the man who was under thirty years old when the year 1999 ended has won all the titles there are in Norway – except the senior title and the one for women, and it will be a long while, if ever, before he wins either of those!

Internationally

- European champion, junior teams
- World champion, junior pairs
- World champion, individual (Generali Masters)
- Several medals in European championships, open teams
- Silver and bronze in the Bermuda Bowl
- Winner of several North American teams and pairs championships
- Several times winner of prestigious invitational tournaments, such as the Cap Gemini in The Hague, the Macallan in London and the Politiken in Copenhagen.
- Bridge Personality of the Year, 1997 (an International Bridge Press Association award)

Some of these triumphs, and other tournaments in which he managed great results, will be mentioned subsequently in later chapters of this book.

Part One

Playing in the Nationals

Reisinger 1998

As mentioned, Geir has for some years been a member of Rita Shugart's team in the US Nationals. They came close to winning many championships, but the first major title did not come until the autumn of 1998, in the Reisinger played in Orlando, Florida.

The Reisinger is the only major US National event that is played with 'board-a-match' ('point-a-board') scoring. That means you either win or lose the board (and score either one or zero) or you share the points. But to draw a board you need to obtain exactly the same score as that at the other table. The size of the difference is immaterial when considering the win/loss. If at your table you play Three No-Trumps and register thirteen tricks, and your opponents bid and make Seven No-Trumps, it produces the win/loss score on the board of 0-1. You can win back that point on the next deal by taking your opponents one down, plus 100, if for instance your team-mates defend against a partscore and concede 90. You win the deal, even though this board would be flat in a normal teams match. There will, of course, be different opinions about the merits of this method of scoring, but what you can say for sure is that it leads to an intense game. All the boards are equally important!

Geir Helgemo is a player who gets great results no matter what kind of tournament he is participating in. He is at the top of the listings in almost every pairs tournament he plays. The prestigious invitational tournaments are normally competed for by pairs, but with IMP scoring, and he has an excellent record in such events. This proves that the type of tournament is not so important – he is bound to be one of the

leaders. However, perhaps his qualities are best suited to pairs, or 'board-a-match'. Small differences – that little extra – are Helgemo's speciality. Because of this, it is no surprise that his first team success in the Nationals came in the Reisinger. 'Board-a-match' could almost have been created for the Norwegian. Some boards from the triumph in 1998 should prove this point.

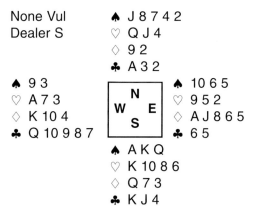

None Vul
Dealer S

```
                ♠ J 8 7 4 2
                ♡ Q J 4
                ◇ 9 2
                ♣ A 3 2
♠ 9 3                          ♠ 10 6 5
♡ A 7 3          N             ♡ 9 5 2
◇ K 10 4      W     E          ◇ A J 8 6 5
♣ Q 10 9 8 7     S             ♣ 6 5
                ♠ A K Q
                ♡ K 10 8 6
                ◇ Q 7 3
                ♣ K J 4
```

The bidding:

West	North	East	South
—	—	—	1♣
Pass	1♠	Pass	2NT
Pass	3NT	All Pass	

Tony Forrester played North and Geir South. The safest contract at teams with the North/South cards is Four Spades. In Three No-Trumps you could easily run into big trouble on a diamond lead. If East puts up his ace and continues the suit, to make his contract declarer must guess the position by playing low to cut the opponents' communications. That line would fail if East held both the ace and king of diamonds, of course. And the defenders could easily defeat the contract by ducking the first trick altogether.

Declarer has only eight tricks, and when he plays on hearts the defenders can cash four diamond tricks and the ace of hearts.

Tony and Geir arrived in Three No-Trumps however, since with flat distributions like theirs the deal could quite often produce the same tricks in no-trumps as the major-suit game. West did not find the diamond lead; he led the ten of clubs, as most of us would have done.

Now declarer has eight top tricks and needs only to steal a heart trick for his contract. It is tough for West to put up his ace of hearts on the first round of the suit and switch to diamonds, as he does not know that this suit is declarer's weak point.

In practice, Geir made it even more difficult for West. Here is what Geir was thinking before he started to play (remember, it was board-a-match scoring): 'Maybe our opponents in the other room have found the best contract, Four Spades. If so, they will lose only two diamonds and a heart. That means I am probably competing against the score of 420 from the other room. In that case there is no great merit in stealing a ninth trick and scoring 400. That will not salvage the board.' While this kind of reasoning is totally flawed at IMPs, it is very often the winning argument at 'board-a-match'. Now witness the delicate art of turning a potential lost board into a win.

The first trick went ten of clubs from West, small from dummy, six of clubs from East, and Geir took the trick with … the king! The illusion was created. West was sure his partner held the jack of clubs since Geir did not take the first trick with it. Then came a heart to dummy's queen, and the four of hearts to the ten and West's ace. Maybe a 'Smith-Peter/oddball' signal from East should have exposed Geir's trickery, but West was caught up in the illusion. He continued

with the queen of clubs! Dummy's ace took the trick and Geir had the communications to cash five spade tricks, three in hearts and three in clubs, for a total of eleven.

The next hand would probably not be worth discussing if it had been played in an IMP match or rubber bridge.

All Vul
Dealer W

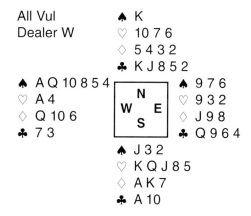

```
              ♠ K
              ♡ 10 7 6
              ♢ 5 4 3 2
              ♣ K J 8 5 2
♠ A Q 10 8 5 4           ♠ 9 7 6
♡ A 4          N         ♡ 9 3 2
♢ Q 10 6    W     E      ♢ J 9 8
♣ 7 3          S         ♣ Q 9 6 4
              ♠ J 3 2
              ♡ K Q J 8 5
              ♢ A K 7
              ♣ A 10
```

The bidding:

West	North	East	South
2♠ (1)	Pass	Pass	Dble
Pass	3♣	Pass	3♡
Pass	4♡	All Pass	

(1) 10–12 HCP, 6-card suit

The Four Heart game looks to be the standard contract, though there may be problems in the play. Declarer needs to ruff the spades and therefore he cannot draw trumps. So, even though Helgemo got a club lead which gave him a trick, it was not a trick he could easily cash.

At trick one Geir put in the eight of clubs from dummy. His intention was to get an idea if clubs were splitting 5–1 or 4–2. When holding five cards people often play small in such a situation, because they can see there is no need to put in the nine. Although this is also the case with the actual holding, for many players it feels more natural to put in the nine from a four-card suit. This play was

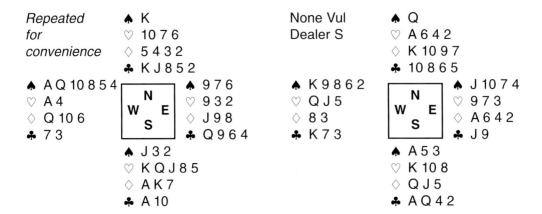

Repeated for convenience

♠ K
♡ 10 7 6
◇ 5 4 3 2
♣ K J 8 5 2

♠ A Q 10 8 5 4
♡ A 4
◇ Q 10 6
♣ 7 3

♠ 9 7 6
♡ 9 3 2
◇ J 9 8
♣ Q 9 6 4

♠ J 3 2
♡ K Q J 8 5
◇ A K 7
♣ A 10

None Vul
Dealer S

♠ Q
♡ A 6 4 2
◇ K 10 9 7
♣ 10 8 6 5

♠ K 9 8 6 2
♡ Q J 5
◇ 8 3
♣ K 7 3

♠ J 10 7 4
♡ 9 7 3
◇ A 6 4 2
♣ J 9

♠ A 5 3
♡ K 10 8
◇ Q J 5
♣ A Q 4 2

not a big deal on the actual hand, but is an example of how Helgemo is trying to find out more about the hand all the time. He collects information, not necessarily reliable information, but indications that may be processed to form the basis for decisions later.

The ten of clubs won trick one. Then followed a spade to West's ace, and West returned the six of diamonds (3rd & 5th) to the jack from East and declarer's king. Geir could have ruffed his spade losers and collected his ten tricks for a score of 620, but he knew that this would probably be the result at the other table and so he went for more than the half point a flat board would give.

The bidding and play pointed to West being 6-2-3-2. After taking the diamond switch in hand Geir did not take a spade ruff. He boldly played the jack of hearts. West walked straight into the trap and played low. Then came a spade ruff, followed by a club to the ace, another spade ruff, and finally the king of clubs for a diamond discard. West had no more clubs, but could not achieve anything by ruffing with his bare ace. The overtrick was enough to give the Shugart team a win on the board.

We are still in Orlando. On the next hand Geir read the distribution like an open book.

The bidding:

West	North	East	South
—	—	—	1NT (1)
Pass	2♣	Pass	2◇
Pass	2NT	Pass	3NT
All Pass			

(1) 15–17

West led the normal small spade, and dummy's queen gave Geir the first trick. A small diamond was played to the queen. Next came a diamond to the nine and ace. East continued spades and was allowed to win the trick with his jack. Then the seven of spades was played to Geir's ace. He had eight top tricks, and the ninth could come from the club finesse. But there was no hurry.

Geir cashed his two diamond tricks and West needed to find two discards. He could throw a club, but on the last diamond he was in trouble. If he let go a spade declarer could play a club to his queen without risking his contract even if the club finesse failed. Later the club suit would produce the ninth trick since the jack was doubleton. If West threw a heart instead, declarer could cash three tricks in that suit. West saw the problem early and blanked his king of clubs in tempo.

But Helgemo had no problems. He played two top hearts and would have claimed his contract if the queen-jack of hearts had dropped. They did not, so he played a club, East following with the nine. A strange situation had arisen in that there was a more than 50% chance of winning the board by playing the ace. Geir knew West's original distribution had been 5-3-2-3 or 5-2-2-4. If the latter, since East had followed with the nine it was clear that the contract would go down. If Geir took the club finesse, West could give up his two spade winners, instead putting his partner in with a low spade, and East's hand would be high! Two down could easily be a lost board. By playing off the ace of clubs Geir would probably at least share the point for the board if West's original distribution had been 5-2-2-4. If West's hand had started as 5-3-2-3 it was clear he had blanked either the jack or the king of clubs, though throwing two clubs from K-x-x was easier to do, than from J-x-x. From the bidding and play West had good indications that his partner held only two clubs, and if they were, for instance, queen doubleton, pitching clubs would give declarer two extra tricks. By following this reasoning Geir played a club to the ace. When the king fell he was able to make an overtrick, and that meant another board won by Shugart's team.

In the final of the 1998 Reisinger Geir was the only player to make nine tricks in this spade contract:

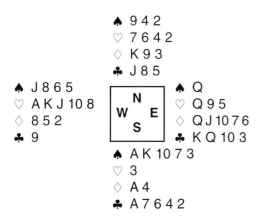

East/West competed vigorously in the auction with their heart fit, but gave up when Geir (South) bid Three Spades. West led his top hearts, the second of which was ruffed by South. Geir now played the ace of clubs and another club. West threw the two of diamonds, and when East cashed another club West let another diamond go. Then came another heart and South ruffed again. His trump holding was now shorter than West's. The ace of diamonds extracted West's last card in that suit, and now Geir played a club on which West threw a heart, as dummy ruffed. A spade to the king collected East's singleton queen, and this was the ending:

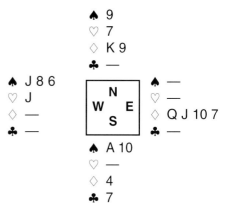

A delicate position, with the defenders having taken three tricks. In the diagram situation Geir played the winning seven of clubs and West was helpless. If he throws his remaining heart, declarer can either discard, or even ruff the club with the nine of spades. Then on the next trick a diamond is played and West must ruff before being forced to play into South's A-10 of spades. If West ruffs high when the seven of clubs is played, he must next choose between two ways of giving declarer the three last tricks and his contract. If West plays a spade, declarer can draw the remaining trump and win the king of diamonds at trick thirteen. And finally, if West ruffs high and plays his jack of hearts, it will be ruffed in dummy while declarer throws his four of diamonds, the last two tricks going to declarer's two high trumps.

The next hand demonstrates a dilemma. While at any form of teams you never know for sure what has happened in the other room, at 'board-a-match' it can be even more important to guess correctly about such matters.

None Vul
Dealer W

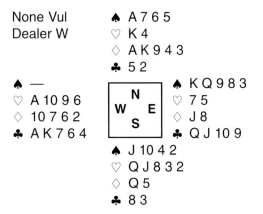

```
                 ♠ A 7 6 5
                 ♡ K 4
                 ◇ A K 9 4 3
                 ♣ 5 2
 ♠ —                          ♠ K Q 9 8 3
 ♡ A 10 9 6          N        ♡ 7 5
 ◇ 10 7 6 2     W       E     ◇ J 8
 ♣ A K 7 6 4         S        ♣ Q J 10 9
                 ♠ J 10 4 2
                 ♡ Q J 8 3 2
                 ◇ Q 5
                 ♣ 8 3
```

The bidding:

West	North	East	South
	Tony		*Geir*
1♣	1◇	1♠	Dble
Pass	1NT	2♣	Pass
Pass	Dble	Pass	2♡
3♣	3♡	Pass	Pass
Dble	All Pass		

The double of One Spade showed hearts – and was not an underbid! It was good work by Forrester to compete again over the opponents' Two Clubs. But maybe Three Hearts on the next round was pushing a bit too hard? Board-a-match scoring produces more penalty doubles of partscores than when playing IMPs.

West was surely optimistic about getting a nice number from Three Hearts doubled, and would probably have doubled at IMPs as well.

Against Three Hearts doubled West took his two club tricks before switching to a small diamond. Geir played low from dummy and East wrongly put in his jack. There followed a trump to the king and another trump to the queen and ace. West continued diamonds and Geir had reached the moment of truth.

If he rose with the ace of diamonds, he could cash the king of diamonds and ruff a diamond. He would then cash the jack of hearts and play a spade. It would not benefit West to ruff, so dummy would score the ace of spades and lead his established fifth diamond, thus ensuring a trick for his eight of hearts. That would be eight tricks. If he could be sure that his team-mates had been left in Three Clubs in the other room, one down would be enough to win the hand, because they would easily score plus 110 or 130. In that case one down in Three Hearts doubled would be as good as making the contract! Alternatively, Geir could finesse the nine of diamonds, discard three spades on the diamond winners and make his contract! However, if the diamond finesse failed, this line would be so expensive it would be certain to be a lost board.

East's play of the jack looked a little strange. Was it a Greek gift? After mature consideration Geir called for the nine of diamonds and made his contract. Was it necessary? Yes, it was. Geir's team-mates had had one of their few terrible boards in the whole of the Reisinger final on this very deal. They had ended up in a bad Two Spade contract on the East/West cards, down three.

Geir's team-mates

Needless to say, Geir was not the only one in the team who played brilliantly in this tournament. He was rescued on several occasions by his team-mates' good bidding and play.

Shugart's team had done well on several occasions in recent Nationals. In 1996 they nearly won the Reisinger; the final margin was as close as possible. A Two Club contract played by Shugart's team on the last board was made, plus 90. That was probably the correct result, but imperfect defence had given declarer a chance to grab an overtrick for plus 110, which he failed to take. At the other table the Shugart team also bought the contract, on this occasion in Two Spades. The contract was doomed against accurate defence so the result should have been minus 100. In a perfect world 'Shugart' would have lost the board by the minimum margin: 90 versus 100. But at that table also the defence fell from grace. Declarer was given some chances to bring home the contract, but failed. Thus both results were normal, even in the not-so-perfect world! If either the Two Club contract had made with an overtrick, or the Two Spade contract had been made, the Shugart team would have won the Reisinger; but in fact that single board meant the difference between first and third place. Third place in such a class tournament should not be regarded as a failure, but that time it was a disappointing bronze medal.

Two years later the team emerged with their first win. All four players played well through the whole event. Here you will see how Rita Shugart rescued Helgemo from an excess of optimism in the semi-final.

NS Vul
Dealer W

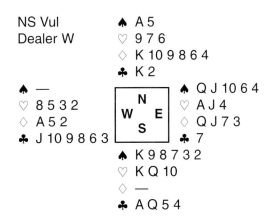

```
              ♠ A 5
              ♡ 9 7 6
              ◇ K 10 9 8 6 4
              ♣ K 2
♠ —                        ♠ Q J 10 6 4
♡ 8 5 3 2         N        ♡ A J 4
◇ A 5 2       W     E      ◇ Q J 7 3
♣ J 10 9 8 6 3     S       ♣ 7
              ♠ K 9 8 7 3 2
              ♡ K Q 10
              ◇ —
              ♣ A Q 5 4
```

The bidding:

Table 1:

West	North	East	South
Helgemo		*Forrester*	
Pass	2◇ (1)	Pass	2♠
3♣	Pass	Pass	Dble
All Pass			

(1) weak

Note that Forrester did not overcall Two Spades over the weak-Two bid even though he was non-vulnerable. That is good bridge judgement, since his four-card diamond suit made the hand dangerous. Moreover, his partner was a passed hand. With four clubs instead of four diamonds I am sure he would have bid Two Spades. But his good judgement did not help much this time. West's Three Club bid would not meet with approval in any textbook. He went three down, doubled, for a deserved minus 500.

Much of the time this would not have been too bad, because North/South have sufficient high-card values to make game with a luckier lie of the cards. But this time Four Spades was impossible to make, so Geir and Tony expected to lose the board.

Repeated
for
convenience

```
             ♠ A 5
             ♡ 9 7 6
             ◇ K 10 9 8 6 4
             ♣ K 2
♠ —                        ♠ Q J 10 6 4
♡ 8 5 3 2        N         ♡ A J 4
◇ A 5 2     W       E      ◇ Q J 7 3
♣ J 10 9 8 6 3    S        ♣ 7
             ♠ K 9 8 7 3 2
             ♡ K Q 10
             ◇ —
             ♣ A Q 5 4
```

Table 2:

West	North	East	South
	Robson		*Shugart*
Pass	2◇	Pass	2♠
3♣!	3♠	Dble	All Pass

Note that East passed over Two Diamonds at this table as well, and again West perpetrated the Three Club overcall. But here Robson raised to Three Spades with his maximum weak Two hand. He was surely looking for a vulnerable game, and probably also liked his well-placed club king very much. East was now happy that he had passed over Two Diamonds – and must have though that Christmas had come early, in the middle of November.

Rita Shugart

But Rita brought home her doubled contract easily. The jack of clubs was led to dummy's king. She then correctly led a heart to her king and laid down the ace of clubs. East could ruff, but that was with a trump trick. Rita could later ruff her losing club with dummy's small trump, and East's overruff was with a trump trick. Declarer was in control and had time to play hearts one more time towards her hand. (The defence cannot lead trumps twice without sacrificing a natural trump trick). Three trump tricks and one heart was all the defenders could manage; plus 730 North/South, and a surprising win of the board for Helgemo and Forrester.

On the next board it was Andy Robson's time to strive for that little extra.

```
             ♠ 9 2
             ♡ A J 8 6 3
             ◇ A Q 9
             ♣ A 7 2
♠ 10                       ♠ 7 5 4
♡ 10 2          N          ♡ K Q 7
◇ 10 8 6 5 4 3  W     E    ◇ J 8
♣ J 8 6 3         S        ♣ K Q 9 5 4
             ♠ A K Q J 8 6 3
             ♡ 9 5 4
             ◇ K 2
             ♣ 10
```

Alan Sontag and Peter Weichsel had bid brilliantly to Six No-Trumps, but Andy and Rita ended up in Six Spades. Since there were the same twelve tricks in both spades and no-trumps, it would normally have been a lost board. However, Andy did not settle for twelve tricks. Unusually for players at this level, the opponents misdefended when he ran his spades and were pseudo-squeezed! Thirteen tricks meant a won board for the Shugart team.

The partner

When Geir Helgemo was selected as Bridge Personality of the Year (1997), the International Bridge Press Association (IBPA) had many reasons for making their choice. One of the explanations they gave was Geir's sympathetic behaviour both as an opponent and as a partner. He deserves those words. He really is a nice partner, but when he plays too much with the same person he can get a little frustrated if the points start flying away. The reason is that almost nobody can play at his level, or rather, nobody can be completely on his wavelength.

I played with him for more than three years, both in Norway and internationally, and he never shouted at me. From time to time he had reason to; after all, he is a human being! But Geir's way of expressing his dissatisfaction is to be calm and quiet, unlike many other players. I learned to take it; I had to. The only other alternative was to play perfect bridge, and I could never quite manage that…

Being Geir's partner varied from being in a bridge heaven where beautiful bridge took place, to feeling lousy because I had broken the bubble of happiness we had temporarily been inside.

Once a comic incident happened when we were playing in the Norwegian Pairs Championship. As always, Geir and his partner were the big favourites, but I had one of my really bad tournaments. It became too much for him on the last round of a session of disasters. I played a partscore in hearts – quite a good contract, in fact. But a slip of the hand (or head) blew away one trick. Then, in the ending I had to guess clubs, a guess that would not have been necessary if the earlier blunder had not happened. I needed to guess right to bring home my Two Heart contract but,

of course, I went one down. Approximately half of the field scored 110, and the rest 140. Naturally Geir was frustrated, not just because of my play in Two Hearts. He could keep silent no longer. At the time I was not yet forty years old, and still had ambitions left in bridge. So Geir's sarcasm was quite cutting when he said: 'You might well have made a trick more when you were still in your prime.' He then went to the men's room, but on coming back some minutes later he apologised.

That is the way it should be, I think. When the stress becomes too much, you should be allowed to release some of it – but not in too nasty a way. After this incident Geir and I played better, both with a little smile on our faces.

Helgemo is normally a kind person when discussing team-mates and partners. But, of course, a player with his skill will very seldom be 100% satisfied. He likes the bridge of his team-mates Rita and Andy, but I have only heard him use the word brilliant about his own partner a few

Tony Forrester

times. The players who have earned that praise are Tor Helness and Tony Forrester. See how Forrester proved his skill in the qualifying stages of the 1998 Reisinger.

None Vul
Dealer W

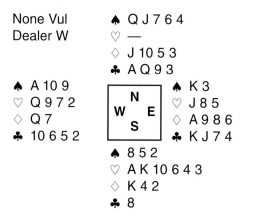

♠ Q J 7 6 4
♡ —
◇ J 10 5 3
♣ A Q 9 3

♠ A 10 9
♡ Q 9 7 2
◇ Q 7
♣ 10 6 5 2

♠ K 3
♡ J 8 5
◇ A 9 8 6
♣ K J 7 4

♠ 8 5 2
♡ A K 10 6 4 3
◇ K 4 2
♣ 8

The bidding:

West	North	East	South
Jacobs	*Helgemo*	*Katz*	*Forrester*
Pass	1♠	Dble	2♡
Dble	All Pass		

Note Ralph Katz's aggressive take-out double of One Spade. I like it, especially since he was not vulnerable. It is often better to stick your head in early – and say your piece early – than wait and have to decide whether to push partner into a contract at the three level. Forrester had the courage to stay in his doubled contract instead of running to Two Spades. He thought his partner would be void in hearts, but from the bidding he could expect the suit to be 4-3.

West led the queen of diamonds, which was allowed to run to the king. Then came the top hearts and a third round of the suit. East unblocked his jack on the second round so West could win the third heart with the nine and take the fourth trick with the queen of hearts. He now switched to a little club to dummy's ace, and Forrester played

the jack of diamonds to East's ace. East continued with another diamond and dummy was in again. Now Forrester played East for a doubleton spade honour by leading the queen from dummy. Katz ducked, and Jacobs as West won his ace and returned a club. Forrester ruffed, then ducked a spade to Katz, and won the last two tricks with a trump and the jack of spades in dummy. This was a winning board, the opponents at the other table playing in a spade partscore making nine tricks.

Good judgement in the bidding by Forrester gave the Shugart team another point on this board. He held as South, vulnerable against not:

♠ K Q J 9
♡ K 10
◇ A 7 6 5
♣ A 9 5

After two passes East opened One Diamond. What would you bid with the South hand?

South has the strength and distribution for a strong no-trump overcall. That was what happened in the other room. North responded with a Two Diamond transfer, and in due course South arrived in Three No-Trumps. This was the full deal:

NS Vul
Dealer W

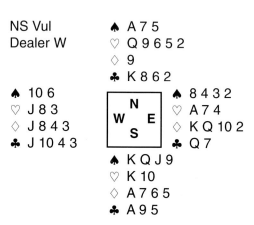

♠ A 7 5
♡ Q 9 6 5 2
◇ 9
♣ K 8 6 2

♠ 10 6
♡ J 8 3
◇ J 8 4 3
♣ J 10 4 3

♠ 8 4 3 2
♡ A 7 4
◇ K Q 10 2
♣ Q 7

♠ K Q J 9
♡ K 10
◇ A 7 6 5
♣ A 9 5

After a diamond lead Three No-Trumps just made nine tricks. However, Tony Forrester did better.

The bidding:

West	North	East	South
Pass	Pass	1♦	1♠!
Pass	2♦	Pass	2NT
Pass	4♠	All Pass	

A simple overcall at the one level with 17 HCP and a four-card suit is unusual, but in this case it was a good decision. The hand's distribution and strength is right for a One No-Trump overcall, but South's diamond stopper is lousy, and with only two hearts it would not be a good idea to double for take out. Once Tony made the overcall he was soon headed for Four Spades, an excellent contract.

A diamond was led to the ace, and Tony immediately ruffed a diamond and played a heart to the king followed by the ten of hearts, which was allowed to run to East's ace. Now he could make twelve tricks in many ways, and he had no problems in doing so. The club shift was taken by the ace, and a diamond was ruffed with the trump ace before declarer drew all the trumps. Later, dummy's hearts were sure to provide at least eleven tricks, and the 3-3 split in fact gave Tony all of the remaining tricks.

As already mentioned, overtricks are extremely important playing 'board-a-match'. That gives the defenders opportunities to help declarer along the wrong route.

On the next deal, where Three No-Trumps was the contract all round the room, we shall see Tony and Geir co-operating well to push declarer over the edge. Both needed to be on the ball to succeed.

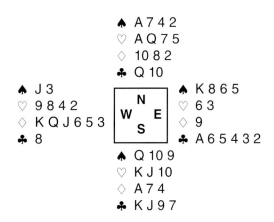

♠ A 7 4 2
♡ A Q 7 5
♦ 10 8 2
♣ Q 10

♠ J 3
♡ 9 8 4 2
♦ K Q J 6 5 3
♣ 8

♠ K 8 6 5
♡ 6 3
♦ 9
♣ A 6 5 4 3 2

♠ Q 10 9
♡ K J 10
♦ A 7 4
♣ K J 9 7

Since the club ace was not with the diamond length, the contract was safe. Like every other West, Tony Forrester led the king of diamonds which declarer allowed to hold the trick. The next diamond was taken by declarer's ace as East pitched a club. South now played on clubs and Geir let him make the first two tricks, but took the third one and cleared the suit. He had thus established a trick for himself in the suit, but apparently in vain because declarer had nine top tricks.

It is hard to see how the defenders could give declarer a problem here. However, Forrester's creativity turned a dull board into a nightmare for declarer. West had to make three discards on the clubs and he let go his three little diamonds. Four heart tricks followed and Geir discarded two spades. This was the position:

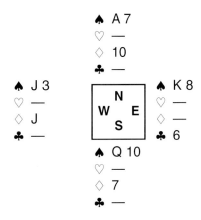

♠ A 7
♡ —
♦ 10
♣ —

♠ J 3
♡ —
♦ J
♣ —

♠ K 8
♡ —
♦ —
♣ 6

♠ Q 10
♡ —
♦ 7
♣ —

Declarer called for the ten of diamonds from dummy. He had endplayed Forrester, who was known to have only one diamond left, to lead a spade. This could not have happened had Forrester not discarded so many diamonds. If the jack and king of spades were interchanged, South would have been his team's hero on this deal. But he was soon disappointed.

Geir had not fallen asleep, and he understood what Tony was up to. On the ten of diamonds Geir discarded the eight of spades. Forrester now had to play a spade, and declarer called for dummy's seven. So East took the last two tricks with his now bare king of spades and a club. Dummy's ace of spades never took a trick, and this magic one down gave the Shugart team the point for the board.

My final example from the 1998 Reisinger triumph is an assassination. Geir Helgemo has had several clashes at the bridge table with Zia Mahmood. Zia and Geir are very good friends with considerable admiration for each other's bridge. Personally speaking, Zia is my favourite of the world's bridge stars, maybe sharing that place with the Americans, Bobby Wolff and Bob Hamman. This personal ranking is based not only on their obvious bridge skills, but also on more personal qualities such as humour, modesty and other things. I do not know Zia very well, but enough to be sure that he will forgive me for recounting the following board (and a few others later on in the book), where he did not fare too well.

This one happened in the Reisinger semi-finals.

NS Vul
Dealer E

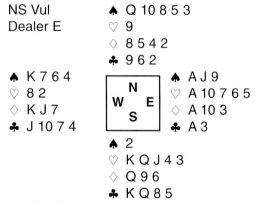

♠ Q 10 8 5 3
♡ 9
◇ 8 5 4 2
♣ 9 6 2

♠ K 7 6 4
♡ 8 2
◇ K J 7
♣ J 10 7 4

♠ A J 9
♡ A 10 7 6 5
◇ A 10 3
♣ A 3

♠ 2
♡ K Q J 4 3
◇ Q 9 6
♣ K Q 8 5

The bidding:

West	North	East	South
Forrester	*Rosenberg*	*Helgemo*	*Zia*
—	—	1NT	2♡
Dble	All Pass		

Helgemo's One No-Trump opening was very much at the top of his normal no-trump range (15–17). Geir's style is to upgrade no-trump hands to the next range when he is a point short but has a good five-card suit. In this case he had three tens, but the suit was a little too weak for such an upgrade. If the suit is as good as A-Q-10-x-x he would often open One No-Trump with 14 HCP, or Two No-Trumps with 19. Hopefully, the good suit will compensate for the shortage of points.

If Geir had opened One Heart his team would have lost the board, since Zia's team-mates had a good result, making eleven tricks in Three No-Trumps. Luckily, Geir opened One No-Trump and, when Zia overcalled Two Hearts, Tony Forrester doubled for take-out. But there was no take-out this time; Geir passed happily.

Even though the jack of clubs was not the best lead for the defence, when the smoke had cleared it was 1100 for East/West.

Part Two

Declarer Play

World-class play

We stay in the fairly recent past. Early on in the year, two of the most prestigious invitational tournaments in the world are played: the Cap Gemini in The Hague and the Macallan in London. Sixteen world-class pairs compete and in recent years Geir has played with Tor Helness with great success. This delightful hand comes from the 1999 Cap Gemini:

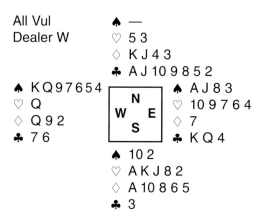

```
All Vul          ♠ —
Dealer W         ♡ 5 3
                 ◇ K J 4 3
                 ♣ A J 10 9 8 5 2

♠ K Q 9 7 6 5 4         ♠ A J 8 3
♡ Q              N      ♡ 10 9 7 6 4
◇ Q 9 2       W     E   ◇ 7
♣ 7 6            S      ♣ K Q 4

                 ♠ 10 2
                 ♡ A K J 8 2
                 ◇ A 10 8 6 5
                 ♣ 3
```

The bidding:

West	North	East	South
	Helness		*Helgemo*
3♠	4♣	4♠	Dble
Pass	4NT	Pass	6◇
All Pass			

South's double of Four Spades showed strength and was not for penalties. In positions where the opponents pre-empt after finding a fit, a double should show general values because with good distribution it is usually better to bid on than try to penalise the opponents.

In this case North's bid of Four No-Trumps showed diamonds, typically a 4-6 or 4-7 hand. That was exactly what Geir wanted to hear. Six Diamonds was a reasonable choice, and when dummy came down Geir could see his

partnership had reached a good slam. Indeed there were many layouts where it would be possible to win all thirteen tricks, but since it was an IMP tournament the main target was to bring home the contract. The king of spades was led and ruffed in dummy. What now?

One other declarer played in slam and the play began the same way; both declarers played a heart to the ace. When the queen dropped, they played a club to the ace and ruffed a club. The contract – actually all the tricks – can easily be made if trumps are 2-2, simply by playing two rounds of trumps and ruffing another club. But with a 3-1 split in trumps this line does not work as dummy can be forced to ruff spades. The other player in slam chose to play a diamond to the king at this stage. Then he ruffed another club, this time with the ten. If West had overruffed, everything would have been all right. But West correctly refused to overruff. South tried his jack of hearts, but now West ruffed and played another spade. Declarer had to ruff in dummy and could not avoid giving West another trump trick. One down. So, what is the solution on this hand?

The declarer who went down was unlucky, but there was a better line. His problem was caused by dummy's trumps being shortened.

Geir Helgemo also saw that, so he did the shortening himself! After the first club ruff Geir played his ten of spades, ruffing in dummy, and then ruffed another club with his six of diamonds. He ruffed so low because he wanted to be overruffed! It could not help West much to overruff though, so he discarded a spade. But Geir was in control, and now played the jack of hearts. West still did not want to ruff (best defence) so he discarded another spade. But next Geir ruffed a small heart and continued with the king of diamonds. Finally a good club was played, on which Helgemo pitched his last small heart from hand. All the defence could get was one trump trick.

The key to success on this hand was a mixture of accurate card reading and some assumptions about probability. Declarer could count on West holding seven spades, and the queen of hearts was surely a singleton. Even at this level of bridge, false-carding with a doubleton queen would be a highly unusual play. Such a manoeuvre could easily give declarer a trick, and perhaps his contract. Then, when East followed to two rounds of clubs, declarer 'knew' West held two or three trumps. If he had two diamonds the contract would be made without any great problems. But if West held three trumps declarer had to be careful. When the ten of spades was ruffed, and a second small club played from dummy, Geir got the message he had been hoping for: West had been dealt three trumps! Helgemo's line of play would have failed only if trumps were splitting 2-2 and West's original distribution had been the very unlikely (from the bidding) 8-1-2-2.

Another unlikely possibility was that West had false-carded with a doubleton queen of hearts. But if that were the case, when Geir played the jack of hearts, West's second heart would have come to light. Of course, you could speculate about West having more than two hearts, but that possibility lies in fantasy land.

Making this contract was worth 15 IMPs, while one down would have been minus 7 IMPs; valuable points to collect in a tournament where Helgemo and Helness were struggling a bit, but eventually finished fourth. Still, their final standing meant they qualified for the next Cap Gemini in the year 2000.

This next hand has a similar theme:

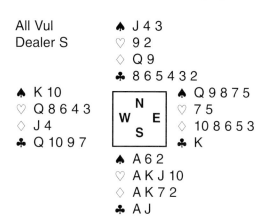

All Vul
Dealer S

	♠ J 4 3
	♡ 9 2
	◇ Q 9
	♣ 8 6 5 4 3 2

♠ K 10
♡ Q 8 6 4 3
◇ J 4
♣ Q 10 9 7

♠ Q 9 8 7 5
♡ 7 5
◇ 10 8 6 5 3
♣ K

♠ A 6 2
♡ A K J 10
◇ A K 7 2
♣ A J

The bidding:

West	North	East	South
—	—	—	2♣
Pass	2◇	Pass	2NT
Pass	3NT	All Pass	

West led a small heart to Helgemo's ten. He had eight top tricks, but it is not easy to see where to get the ninth. The club suit might produce some tricks but it seems impossible to reach them. Even if clubs split 3-2, the queen of diamonds has to be used up in order to establish the suit, and later, although the clubs will be good for three tricks, there is no entry to them.

The solution is difficult to spot, but you have to consider playing the suit your opponents have led. Geir's decision at trick two was simply to play three rounds of hearts! He had taken the first three tricks, while setting up two tricks for his opponents. He then allowed West to cash his hearts. West took his queen and then the thirteenth heart (an unsound idea since he was doing what Helgemo wanted him to do and squeezing his partner). East was now starting to feel the pinch, since he had been forced to discard three times. First he pitched two little spades, and then a diamond. Geir pitched some clubs from dummy and a spade from his hand. After the hearts West tried a club to East's king and South ... followed with the jack! Then East switched to a spade, which went round to West's king. This was the ending:

to four cards, and could not keep four diamonds as well as the queen of spades.

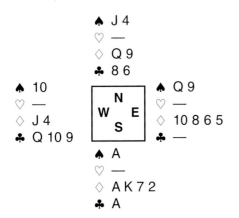

Thinking about the end position

The defenders had four tricks, so Geir needed the rest. West played the ten of spades which was won by South's ace. Now came the ace of clubs and East had to find a discard. He had to come down

Technical play

We now move to Ålesund, a town on the west coast of Norway where a team tournament is played once a year. Geir Helgemo has often played in this tournament, and his team has won it several times. This deal could have been taken straight from a bridge textbook.

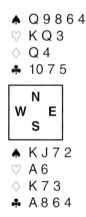

♠ Q 9 8 6 4
♡ K Q 3
◇ Q 4
♣ 10 7 5

♠ K J 7 2
♡ A 6
◇ K 7 3
♣ A 8 6 4

The bidding:

West	North	East	South
			Helgemo
—	—	—	1NT
Pass	2♡ (1)	Pass	2♠
Pass	3NT	Pass	4♠
All Pass			
(1) transfer			

Because of the transfer sequence, South became declarer in Four Spades. The contract was touch and go, and looking at only the North/South cards it is difficult to believe declarer can avoid four losers. Try it for yourself before looking at the complete deal.

In addition to the trump and diamond aces it looks as if there are two club losers, since only one of South's three little clubs can be discarded on hearts. West led the king of clubs, which was allowed to hold, and continued the suit to the jack and ace.

Geir played the jack of spades, and then followed with the king of spades when East did not take the first round of trumps. Both opponents followed suit the first time, then on the second round East took his trump ace while West discarded a heart. East now exited with his last trump; obviously he had no more clubs. Declarer won the third round of spades with dummy's queen. Can you see what he needed to hope for to make the contract? This was the ending:

♠ 9 8
♡ K Q 3
◇ Q 4
♣ 10

♠ 7
♡ A 6
◇ K 7 3
♣ 8 6

The four of diamonds was played from the dummy. If West held the ace of diamonds there was no hope, because he would be able to cash his club queen, the setting trick. So the ace of diamonds had to be with East, and indeed it was. It would not have helped East to put up the ace, because if he did, the king of diamonds would later provide a discard for dummy's remaining club loser. So Geir's king of diamonds took the trick. Next followed three rounds of hearts with declarer discarding a diamond. Finally, declarer exited with a diamond, endplaying East with his ace. He had to play a red suit (in fact diamonds, as he was out of hearts), and declarer could ruff in hand and discard dummy's last club. This was the full deal:

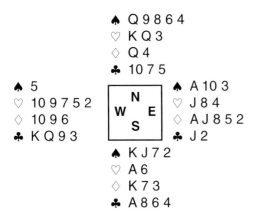

```
              ♠ Q 9 8 6 4
              ♡ K Q 3
              ◇ Q 4
              ♣ 10 7 5
♠ 5                          ♠ A 10 3
♡ 10 9 7 5 2      N          ♡ J 8 4
◇ 10 9 6       W     E       ◇ A J 8 5 2
♣ K Q 9 3         S          ♣ J 2
              ♠ K J 7 2
              ♡ A 6
              ◇ K 7 3
              ♣ A 8 6 4
```

Åse Langeland

This play, where East was offered a choice of unpalatable alternatives, is known as Morton's Fork. Note that West could have broken up the position by switching to a diamond at trick two.

We move now to warm Rimini, Italy. In March 2000 Geir played in the European Mixed Pairs there, partnering Åse Langeland from Alta, Norway. They did well for a while, but a few poor rounds in the final left them in twelfth place. On this hand from the first session of the final Geir used pressure to solve his problem.

```
EW Vul            ♠ 8 2
Dealer W          ♡ K Q 10
                  ◇ A J 8 6
                  ♣ 10 9 5 2
♠ J 9 7 6                    ♠ A 10 4
♡ J 5 4 2         N          ♡ 9 8 6
◇ Q 4 2        W     E       ◇ 10 9 5 3
♣ K 6             S          ♣ 7 4 3
                  ♠ K Q 5 3
                  ♡ A 7 3
                  ◇ K 7
                  ♣ A Q J 8
```

The bidding:

West	North	East	South
Rand	*Langeland*	*Waksman*	*Helgemo*
Pass	Pass	Pass	1♣
Pass	1◇	Pass	2NT
Pass	3NT	All Pass	

Nissan Rand led a spade to East's ace and a second spade was taken by Helgemo who played a heart to dummy and took a losing club finesse. Rand cleared the spades. Now Helgemo had ten top tricks. Many other declarers took the diamond finesse and made their eleventh trick rather luckily. Geir played better, and, assuming West had the fourth spade, would have made his extra trick either if West had the queen of diamonds or if East had queen doubleton.

This is how Helgemo continued: he cashed his club winners on which West threw two hearts. Now the remaining two hearts were cashed and West had to throw one more card on the last one. He couldn't let the spade go, of course, so he threw a diamond. When Geir now cashed his king of diamonds and played a diamond towards dummy there was a show-up-squeeze!

If the queen of diamonds had not shown up in the two-card end-position Geir would have played dummy's ace of diamonds, because West was known to hold a spade winner and so couldn't hold more than one diamond. Three No-Trumps plus two was a good score, but on a luckier day Geir would have won the eleventh trick by dropping the doubleton queen off side.

The magician

The Norwegian Pairs Championships is played once a year and has often been a scene of great success for Helgemo. At the time of writing he has won it four times as well as finishing in the top three on many other occasions. The standard at such tournaments is normally uneven, which gives the better card players the chance to make tricks out of nothing. Normally it is necessary to 'read', or in some cases even to guess, the distribution correctly. Here is an example where I almost felt sorry for West.

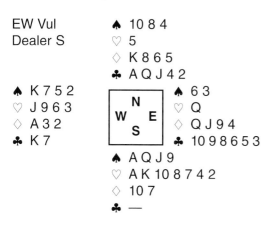

EW Vul
Dealer S

```
              ♠ 10 8 4
              ♡ 5
              ◇ K 8 6 5
              ♣ A Q J 4 2
♠ K 7 5 2              ♠ 6 3
♡ J 9 6 3      N      ♡ Q
◇ A 3 2    W     E    ◇ Q J 9 4
♣ K 7          S      ♣ 10 9 8 6 5 3
              ♠ A Q J 9
              ♡ A K 10 8 7 4 2
              ◇ 10 7
              ♣ —
```

Geir as South reached the normal contract of Four Hearts, as did 33 of the 36 tables. There appear to be four losers off the top – two in trumps, with the unfortunate lay-out, and one each in spades and diamonds.

Double-dummy, the best defence is to lead the ace of diamonds and continue the suit. But in practice West, who had a tough lead problem, cannot be criticised for choosing a small spade, which went round to declarer's queen. Geir now cashed his ace of hearts and stared for some time at East's queen. Was this a singleton? He could not know for sure. If the queen-jack of hearts were doubleton everybody would succeed. Geir decided

not to be so optimistic; therefore, he left trumps alone at this stage, and led a diamond. West put up his ace and continued the suit to dummy's king.

Geir's elegant continuation was to ruff a diamond in hand followed by a small (!) trump from hand. West won the trick, but was endplayed with three suits to choose between, all three helping declarer. Spades would give declarer a second cheap trick in that suit, and the last spade loser could be discarded on the ace of clubs. A trump from West would be no better for him, giving up his second trump trick. Finally, his actual choice of a club switch allowed declarer to finesse and take two tricks there, so that he could pitch two spades on the clubs. After this nice play, Geir had only one trump loser left, for ten tricks and a near top.

The next story is true, even though you may not believe it. It happened in the 2000 Generali Masters (the World Individual Championship) in Greece. Geir had won this tournament previously, but when he played this hand he was

Antonio Sementa, winner of the
2000 Generali Masters

struggling at the lower end of the placings. The board represented a turning point and Geir eventually finished ninth.

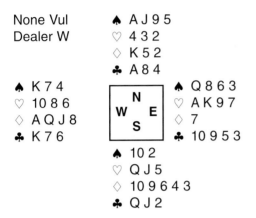

```
None Vul        ♠ A J 9 5
Dealer W        ♡ 4 3 2
                ◇ K 5 2
                ♣ A 8 4
♠ K 7 4                      ♠ Q 8 6 3
♡ 10 8 6         N           ♡ A K 9 7
◇ A Q J 8      W   E         ◇ 7
♣ K 7 6          S           ♣ 10 9 5 3
                ♠ 10 2
                ♡ Q J 5
                ◇ 10 9 6 4 3
                ♣ Q J 2
```

Boye Brogeland

What happened must have been felt like a nightmare for the opponents, the Norwegian Boye Brogeland (West) and the Italian Antonio Sementa. Both were in the upper part of the placings at this stage. This hand does not give full justice to either of them, especially Sementa who played very well in the tournament and eventually took the world title. Brogeland finished in 19th place of the 52 competitors.

The bidding was almost unbelievable itself.

West	North	East	South
1◇	Dble	Rdble	1♡
Pass	Pass	1NT	2♣(!)
Pass	Pass	Dble	Pass
Pass	2♡	Dble	All Pass

Two bids on three-card suits is rather unusual, but that was not the end of this drama. Geir had to declare this silly contract. He needed some help.

The six of hearts was led to East's king. He switched to the seven of diamonds and Geir put in the ten. West covered with his jack and the king took the trick. Now Geir played a heart towards his hand, and East played low, letting declarer win the trick with the queen.

Next came the two of spades from hand, and he played the jack from dummy. This peculiar way of playing the spade suit must have persuaded East that West held K-10 of spades, because he covered the jack with the queen and continued spades. West then covered the ten with his king and dummy's ace won. Geir could cash another spade trick with the nine, before ruffing dummy's last spade with his last trump. West threw a club. Geir already had five tricks and two more were to come from clubs. When he played the jack of clubs West didn't cover and the jack won the trick. Next came the two of clubs and West, who had discarded a club on the spade ruff, followed with his king! Dummy's last trump was played and East should have played low, letting West in to make his diamond tricks. But East rose with the ace and West's cards were dead! East had to give Helgemo another club trick, and eight in total: two spades, one trump, one spade ruff, the diamond king and three(!) clubs. Phew!

Helgemo made Two Hearts doubled when a more common contract throughout the field was Two Hearts, making, in the other direction!

A classic play

Helgemo is a bridge globe-trotter. For those of us who usually play with him in Norway it can be frustrating when he disappears so often, but the frustration is compensated for by the good experience of playing with him when he is home. Strangely, the large number of boards he plays professionally does not affect his standard in less important events. After hectic weeks on the international bridge circuit, he is still often willing to play in private games or small local tournaments. And these games seem to mean as much to him now as they ever did!

The most enjoyable episodes I have had as his partner have been in such 'un-important' bridge events. Even when not playing for money, masterpoints or titles, he expects the standard of bridge to be as high as possible. And this attitude is very valuable. It is essential to create good habits, and avoid 'loco-bridge' just for the fun of it. This is a fact young players should keep in mind.

On one occasion Geir had been abroad collecting some new trophy, and he just had time to leave his suitcase at home before being dragged to the Bridgehouse in Trondheim. He had not been in the room five minutes when this happened:

All Vul   ♠ K 9 2
Dealer N   ♡ A 9 2
           ◇ 10
           ♣ A K J 9 4 2

```
      N
  W       E
      S
```

           ♠ J 4
           ♡ K 8 7
           ◇ K Q 9 7 6
           ♣ 10 7 5

Geir declared Three No-Trumps. The five of diamonds was led and dummy's ten took the first trick. Try to play it yourself before looking below at the East/West cards.

This is a deal that should be played differently at pairs from teams or rubber bridge. At pairs you should maybe try for overtricks. But if clubs are not friendly the contract might be at risk. Since the tournament we were playing in was scored by IMPs it was essential to play safely. After the ten of diamonds holds, if you cash the ace and king of clubs, you are in trouble if the queen does not fall. A third round of clubs sets up the suit, but the opponents can switch to a killing heart. Declarer has only eight tricks and there are terrible communications between the North and South hands. Can you see the solution? This was the full deal:

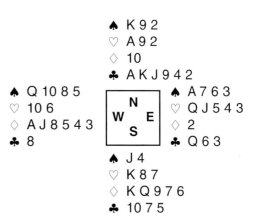

In practice the game contract was wrapped up in no time at all. At trick two Geir simply called for the jack of clubs. Now the defenders could do whatever they wanted, and they could not find any way of giving declarer a problem. He had created entries back to his own hand, to drive out the ace of diamonds and collect another diamond trick, his ninth.

No hope

The best players often score valuable points even when they do not bid to the best contract. Helgemo has shown an amazing ability in such situations, especially in pairs tournaments – where most of the other pairs will have the same difficulty in getting to the right contract. His ability to produce extra tricks is invaluable. The difference between going one or two down can sometimes be greater than bidding a grand slam compared with stopping at the six level.

A typical problem for many players is that they stop trying when they see that their contract will go down. A lot of points are lost because of that, but Geir never gives up.

This deal is from an open pairs final in the Norwegian Championship some years ago:

Lasse Aaseng

```
None Vul        ♠ K 9 7 6 5 2
Dealer W        ♡ Q
                ♢ A K 7
                ♣ A J 4
♠ J 8 3                      ♠ Q 10 4
♡ A J            N           ♡ K 9 8 7
♢ Q 9 5     W        E       ♢ J 10 3
♣ K Q 6 3 2      S           ♣ 10 8 5
                ♠ A
                ♡ 10 6 5 4 3 2
                ♢ 8 6 4 2
                ♣ 9 7
```

The bidding:

West	North	East	South
1NT	Dble	Pass	3♡
Pass	4♡	All Pass	

West opened a 13–15 One No-Trump, and North, Lasse Aaseng, doubled. For once Geir's choice in the bidding was not the best. With the actual lay-out he should have passed out the doubled contract instead of bidding himself. On a spade lead One No-Trump doubled would probably have gone at least two down, and Two Clubs would not have been much cheaper for East/West. But quite naturally Geir bid over his partner's double. Most of us would have tried Two Hearts, whereupon presumably North would have bid Two Spades, ending the auction.

Geir's choice of bid – Three Hearts – showed a weak hand with good distribution, though typically slightly more robust heart intermediates. Admittedly the South hand could easily have produced a lot of tricks if North's support had been better. In this case though, North's support for hearts was lousy, and Aaseng's raise to game seems misguided.

The contract was doomed, of course. From the start there were four trump losers, and one in each of the minor suits. Declarer should normally end up with seven or eight tricks. But Geir brought home nine tricks in approximately as many seconds.

The king of clubs was led and allowed to hold the trick. West switched to a diamond to dummy's ace. Geir played a spade to the ace, took the club finesse and cashed the ace of clubs discarding a diamond. Then he played the king of spades discarding another diamond, followed by ruffing a spade. After that a diamond was played to the king and a diamond ruffed. That was eight tricks and Geir now simply played a trump. Whatever the defenders did, Geir could just wait for his ninth trick in hearts. Maybe he had made an unlucky choice in the bidding, but since several pairs had got too high in spades, one down was almost an average. Scoring points like this is at least as valuable as the points obtained from squeezes, endplays and the like.

In a tournament played back in Trondheim, Geir became the declarer in this Three No-Trump contract:

NS Vul
Dealer S

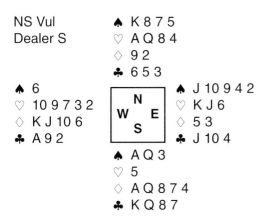

♠ K 8 7 5
♡ A Q 8 4
◇ 9 2
♣ 6 5 3

♠ 6
♡ 10 9 7 3 2
◇ K J 10 6
♣ A 9 2

♠ J 10 9 4 2
♡ K J 6
◇ 5 3
♣ J 10 4

♠ A Q 3
♡ 5
◇ A Q 8 7 4
♣ K Q 8 7

The bidding:

West	North	East	South
—	—	—	1◇
Pass	1♡	Pass	2♣
Pass	2◇	Pass	2NT
Pass	3NT	All Pass	

Quite a normal contract but, as you can see, the lie of the cards is not good for declarer. West tried to hit his partner's strength by leading his singleton spade, but such a lead is unlikely to succeed. East did not overcall One Spade and West has all the entries, thus the lead of a small heart – declarer's likely singleton – would have been the best choice.

The six of spades went to the nine from East, and South took the trick with his queen. Then Geir played a small diamond towards dummy's nine. Wisely, West put up his ten of diamonds and avoided the first disaster. West now switched to his lowest heart. Geir put in the eight of hearts and East won with the jack. Geir took the low spade continuation with his ace, West throwing a heart. Now the king of clubs was played. West took his ace and continued hearts; again he played a small one, hoping declarer would put in the queen. But Geir called for the four of hearts from dummy, and East won his king. Back came another spade from East, and this went to dummy's king. Two heart tricks were cashed, and this was the position with the lead in dummy:

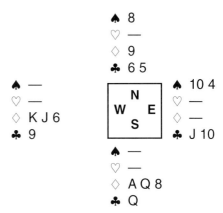

♠ 8
♡ —
◇ 9
♣ 6 5

♠ —
♡ —
◇ K J 6
♣ 9

♠ 10 4
♡ —
◇ —
♣ J 10

♠ —
♡ —
◇ A Q 8
♣ Q

The defenders had already won four tricks, so the contract was doomed. West had been forced to let go a club, because if he had thrown away a diamond Geir could simply have ducked a diamond trick and taken the rest. So West had found the best defence, a fact that gave Geir the chance to go down with honour. He now played a club to the queen, and with only three cards left he played the queen of diamonds from his hand. West had to take it, but he was now forced to lead from his J-6 of diamonds into declarer's A-8.

East/West were not dissatisfied. After all they had beaten Mr Helgemo – 'The One' – through a defence where at least a couple of pitfalls had been avoided. But one down proved to be cheap for North/South, due to the miserable lie of the cards from declarer's perspective. Actually North/South got a 75% score for losing 100.

In pairs tournaments you may often see declarers making desperate attempts to bring home their contracts. Such a strategy can be the right one if you can see that the contract played is so unusual that you need to try to make it as the only way of getting any points at all on the actual deal. However, at pairs there may be a lot to gain by not always being so eager to make your contract, though, of course, this way of thinking is not recommended at teams, where you can earn much more by bringing home your contract than you lose by going an extra one down. However, even at teams you can gain a lot by realising that you are doomed and minimising the loss. One down in a contract can occasionally be a good board. If the lay-out of the cards is terribly unfriendly, from time to time you may find that your opponents in the other room have gone three down or more. The comment you may hear is normally along the following lines: 'I

gave up when I knew I was going down.'

To finish these thoughts I should mention a Three No-Trump contract played in the 1995 European Pairs Championship in Rome. I played with Helgemo, and like everyone else we reached a normal Three No-Trumps. The contract had good prospects at the start. A double finesse in diamonds had to be taken, and if either the jack of diamonds or the king of diamonds was onside, the contract would make. But in practice the contract became much less attractive when the first diamond finesse lost to the jack. That opponent now established his suit, and started twitching. He was excited, it was easy to tell. If the defenders got on lead again, the contract would be defeated by at least two tricks. But if the second diamond finesse was working it meant we could make a vulnerable game.

To take the opponents' excitement and body language into account is something you do at your own risk, but the ability to do so is one of the most important elements of table presence. In Rome, giving up any chance of making the contract and settling for your eight top tricks turned out to be a great success. The deal was played in the qualifying event, and our defenders were disappointed when the score-sheet revealed that one down was a terrible result for them. An almost endless row of 200s and some 300s proved that minus 100 gave us an 88.5% score on the board. In fact it was our best board of the whole session! Playing a European Championship and going down in your game contracts is not exactly what you dream about, but when it gives you almost all the matchpoints it is not too bad, is it?

Solid play

As already mentioned, the everyday game of bridge does not contain all that much potential for masterpieces, but instead it features deals where what is needed is to avoid stupid mistakes – in other words: playing soundly pays!

The day after a local teams match (in which I did not take part) Helgemo and I had a drink together. He gave me a piece of paper with a deal on it. 'How would you play this Three No-Trumps?' he asked. This was the deal:

All Vul   ♠ 10 8 7 2
Dealer S   ♡ Q 9 8
           ◇ 9 8
           ♣ A K 8 3

```
    N
  W   E
    S
```

           ♠ K Q
           ♡ K J 10 2
           ◇ A K 5
           ♣ 9 7 6 2

The bidding:

West	North	East	South
—	—	—	1NT
Pass	2♣	Pass	2♡
Pass	3NT	All Pass	

The four of diamonds was led (3rd & 5th). I was supposed to suggest a line of play. When people give you a problem on paper, often what is needed is a spectacular play. And certainly this contract does not look easy to bring home. Declarer has to knock out the ace of hearts, but then the defenders establish their diamonds.

After some consideration I felt I was able to give him quite an inspired

suggestion. My idea was to take the first diamond. Then play the ten of hearts to the queen, which will hold the trick, I hope. Then a spade to the king, also holding. After that the two of hearts is played towards dummy. Maybe West plays low again? Then another spade towards the closed hand, hoping to steal a trick with the queen of spades. Getting two tricks with a doubleton king-queen has happened before, has it not? After all this, it is time to knock out the ace of hearts, and the contract will make.

Satisfied with myself, I put away the note and concentrated on the drink in front of me. I was thinking that this was how the 'maestro' had played it. But, no. Geir smiled, while admitting that my complex line of play might have worked. But he had, of course, played differently, and better.

The problem on this deal is that you need tricks in both hearts and spades, but have no time for it. The opponents will have their five tricks before declarer can take nine. The solution is to consider playing a suit other than the obvious one – hearts – or the second alternative – clubs.

At trick two Geir played the king of spades, which went to East's ace. Back came a diamond, and West's three told Geir the suit was probably 4-4. That meant the defenders had established two diamond tricks. The ace of hearts was knocked out. West was now on play, and the defence cashed their two diamond tricks. They should not have done so. This was the full deal:

All Vul
Dealer S

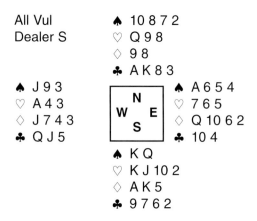

```
                ♠ 10 8 7 2
                ♡ Q 9 8
                ◇ 9 8
                ♣ A K 8 3
♠ J 9 3                        ♠ A 6 5 4
♡ A 4 3         N              ♡ 7 6 5
◇ J 7 4 3     W   E            ◇ Q 10 6 2
♣ Q J 5         S              ♣ 10 4
                ♠ K Q
                ♡ K J 10 2
                ◇ A K 5
                ♣ 9 7 6 2
```

Just as in my line, Geir needed the defence not to be too accurate, although by comparison the defensive slip needed here, that of rectifying the count, was relatively small. But note that if you move the three of spades over to East, and a small heart back, the contract would have been cold with declarer being able to collect three improbable tricks in spades. However, even though that was not the case, nevertheless Geir made his contract. After the defenders had taken their diamonds this was the position:

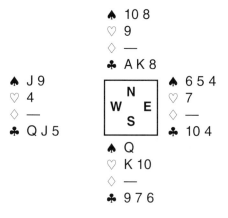

```
                ♠ 10 8
                ♡ 9
                ◇ —
                ♣ A K 8
♠ J 9                          ♠ 6 5 4
♡ 4             N              ♡ 7
◇ —           W   E            ◇ —
♣ Q J 5         S              ♣ 10 4
                ♠ Q
                ♡ K 10
                ◇ —
                ♣ 9 7 6
```

East exited with a heart. Declarer cashed his queen of spades and continued by playing off the remaining heart trick. West had to keep his jack of spades and could no longer hold three clubs. Nine tricks taken, through a simple black-suit squeeze.

What happened on this deal is typical. Geir made his contract by playing straightforwardly, while the rest of the field went down after trying different kinds of spectacular lines (like mine). Many players frequently search for spectacular lines of play. Maybe they believe that is the way Geir collects his points. Perhaps they do so because bridge magazines and newspaper columns very often focus on the fancy deals, and Helgemo has quite often played a leading role in such stories. He is, in fact, a player who has made many spectacular and strange plays, both as declarer and defender, but that does not mean he is searching for squeezes and endplays on every deal!

After having played with him for a while, I was surprised to discover the secret of his success. What usually happened was surprisingly normal, but from time to time everything exploded. And this is part of the secret. The myth of a player who is a magician all the time is, of course, a myth. One should remember that Geir Helgemo is a professional player, playing thousands of deals every year. The reason he so often succeeds is primarily because his game is based on an exceptionally sound technique. This is a very important point to bear in mind, especially for younger talents. Consistency and avoiding unnecessary errors are critical.

In the bidding it is also important to find yourself a style and stick to it. Too many players try to be clever much too often. They are trying to create the situations where they hope to collect some extra points. Trying to hit the bull's eye on every deal is not a good idea at bridge. We all know that it is sometimes right to be aggressive in the bidding, but at other times it is wrong to push so hard, even though the situation and cards look very similar. That is the way bridge is. But changing your style all the time, trying always to hit the right spot, will not do you any good. Of course, when you try to play like this you may win a tournament with an 80% score, but that is probably going to happen once in a lifetime. The normal result will be average, or below.

It is better to find a style you feel comfortable with, and stick to it. The point is, you should believe that your approach to bridge is sound, and that it is going to give you good results in the long run. I can tell you that Geir Helgemo never complains when he loses out on a deal because his style was not the right one for any particular hand.

Also in play and defence the strategy of not creating too many swings all the time is good. Steadiness pays! However, one maxim I have never understood is: 'Do not play against the field.' I guess it was meant to read something like: 'Do not play differently from the field if the odds are too strongly against your action.' If a play has only a very tiny chance of succeeding you should forget about it, even if it is tempting. This is certainly the best strategy when playing pairs, where it is a good idea to settle for a fair share of the matchpoints (if you are in the normal contract), instead of gambling and potentially being left with a zero. However, this approach involves some negative thinking, and you should take the risk of following your own hunch, especially if the play you want to take is only a little worse than the more obvious line of play.

To illustrate this, we are now going back in time to a pairs tournament in Trondheim. Once again the contract is the most popular one, Three No-Trumps.

NS Vul ♠ A Q 8 2
Dealer S ♡ Q 2
  ◊ K J 2
  ♣ Q J 8 5

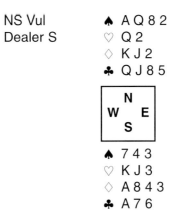

  ♠ 7 4 3
  ♡ K J 3
  ◊ A 8 4 3
  ♣ A 7 6

The bidding:

West	North	East	South
—	—	—	1◊
Pass	1♠	Pass	1NT
Pass	3NT	All Pass	

This was the bidding at most of the tables, and East/West were silent. Where Helgemo was South, West led the five of hearts (3rd & 5th). Dummy's queen took the first trick, while East produced the four, standard count.

This is a deal where you have to choose between a great many lines. A finesse in spades or diamonds might work, but it is also obvious that clubs need to be brought in as well. However, the defenders cannot be given the lead too often, since their heart suit is threatening.

Geir Helgemo found a mildly unusual line of play. He asked for the queen of clubs at trick two. Everyone played small. Then came the key play: the jack of clubs from dummy. East had to cover, Geir took the ace and the ten came down from West. Now Geir could establish another club trick by playing the seven, but then the defenders would give him a heart trick and after that he could not let them in again. Declarer has eight tricks by establishing the third club trick, but he still has the choice between a spade and a diamond finesse. After forcing out the nine of clubs, and being given the second heart trick, he could play either the diamonds or spades from the top, and finesse in the other suit if nothing favourable happened. Of those alternatives, cashing the top diamonds and finessing in spades if the queen of diamonds does not drop is the best line. This is a sound mathematical approach (especially at teams), but makes declarer go one extra down (vulnerable) from time to time. That feels dangerous, especially at matchpoints.

Geir considered the matter for a long time, an unusual event for him. Then rather surprisingly he did not continue playing on clubs despite his early success in the suit. He simply took the diamond finesse; and it worked. Only after he won the trick with the jack of diamonds did he go back to clubs and establish his ninth trick there. This was the full deal:

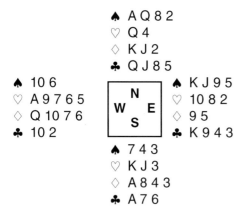

The deal contains an interesting play of the club suit. The reason that Geir did not establish the third club trick at once and guess which finesse to take later was that the contract had some possibilities of making even if the diamond finesse failed. In that case Geir would not have had time to establish the club trick. But he could still come home, by finding the diamonds 3-3 (or perhaps by finessing the eight of

diamonds on some lies of the cards), followed by a successful spade finesse.

It was not a textbook deal, but one containing a mixture of technique and using a good nose. And Geir made the right choice, as he does so often. The play in clubs is a little strange, but probably the best one, mathematically. From the first trick West has been placed with five hearts against East's three. Even though declarer does not know much about the other suits it is a marginally better probability that West is the one (if any) with a doubleton club. When it is the ten or nine doubleton Geir's line of play works. Even if the ten or nine had not dropped on the second round of the suit, declarer could still have changed his strategy and gone for the spades or diamonds.

Deals where Geir Helgemo makes the right choice, when it looks like a guess, are countless. It is certainly no coincidence, but it is not easy to wrest from him the secret of his success. I think it has to do with the small details he collects during the play; in the end they give him some kind of clue as to what to do. It is important to be alert all the time, and then sort out all the hypothetical information before adding it to the known facts about the deal.

Even when Geir was a very young junior player, people noticed his fabulous ability to make the right choices. In the bulletin of the 1990 European Junior Championship, the Norwegian bridge journalist Arne Hofstad mentioned this fact. Arne was the best bridge journalist in Norway for nearly forty years, and highly respected internationally. He won a lot of journalist awards, quite frequently writing about Geir Helgemo. One article from the above-mentioned junior championship is set out below.

The Norwegian junior team at that time had a lot of excellent card players.

They were not at all afraid of following the line they believed to be right, even though the percentage calculators were of a different opinion. A good nose combined with a natural talent for card-playing technique were their qualities. Systems and theoretical knowledge had to be developed later.

The title of Hofstad's article was 'The Norwegians have it at their fingertips'. He won the championship journalist award for it, and Geir won the prize for 'Best Played Hand'. Geir has later stressed that he felt his play did not deserve any prize, since it was all about sniffing out the vibrations at the table. However, he agreed that Hofstad deserved the prize for his good article. This is the full story:

All Vul
Dealer S

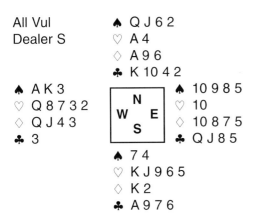

♠ Q J 6 2
♡ A 4
♢ A 9 6
♣ K 10 4 2

♠ A K 3
♡ Q 8 7 3 2
♢ Q J 4 3
♣ 3

♠ 10 9 8 5
♡ 10
♢ 10 8 7 5
♣ Q J 8 5

♠ 7 4
♡ K J 9 6 5
♢ K 2
♣ A 9 7 6

The bidding:

West	North	East	South
—	—	—	1♡
Pass	1♠	Pass	2♣
Pass	2♢ (1)	Pass	2NT
Pass	3NT	All Pass	

(1) 4th suit, forcing to game.

When you see the line of play Geir selected, you might imagine that West gave the game away in the bidding, by hesitating, by questioning, or something. But he had done nothing of the sort, and part of Helgemo's play on this deal must be placed in the category of pure intuition.

West led the three of diamonds and Geir took the first trick with the king. Then, with a steady hand, he played the jack of hearts which held the trick! East's ten was a joy to see, and next Geir played a club to the king and the ten of clubs from dummy. East covered and was allowed to hold the trick. Back came a diamond which went to West's jack, and the next diamond went to dummy's ace. Now Geir cashed the ace of hearts before playing a club for the marked finesse through East. This was the ending:

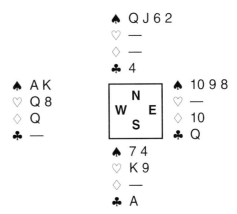

♠ Q J 6 2
♡ —
♢ —
♣ 4

♠ A K
♡ Q 8
♢ Q
♣ —

♠ 10 9 8
♡ —
♢ 10
♣ Q

♠ 7 4
♡ K 9
♢ —
♣ A

When Geir played the ace of clubs the situation was not pleasant for West. He might just as well have folded up his cards and conceded. He had to keep two hearts, and whether he pitched the queen of diamonds or a spade honour he would be endplayed in spades. At trick twelve a heart lead into Geir's K-9 was the beautiful finale.

More technique

In Copenhagen, there is a biennial prestigious invitational tournament called the Politiken World Pairs. On this deal from that event Helgemo was playing with Helness. It demonstrates a simple, but fine technique.

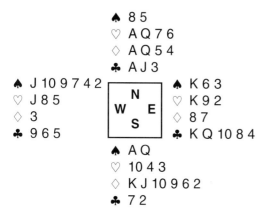

Three No-Trumps was the best game contract, but after an optimistic slam try Tor and Geir unfortunately ended up in Five Diamonds. The tournament was played with IMP scoring so as long as Geir could bring home the contract it did not matter much that they had missed the ideal spot of Three No-Trumps.

The jack of spades was led and Geir took the first trick. He cashed his second

Krzysztof Martens

spade before drawing trumps ending in dummy. Now he played the three of clubs. East put up the ten and continued with his king of clubs, which went to the ace. This was the ending:

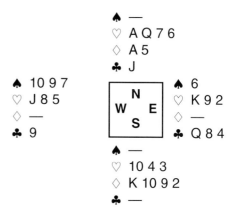

The final coup was simple, but elegant. The jack of clubs was played from dummy and East had to cover with his queen, which was allowed to hold the trick as Geir pitched the three of hearts. East was endplayed and had to play a black suit for a ruff and discard, or lead into dummy's heart tenace. Two club tricks were all the defence could get, and a potential loss on the deal was avoided.

As you can see, once Geir attacked clubs before hearts, the defence was helpless, since neither defender can lead hearts without giving up a trick in that suit.

The following year Geir played in this tournament with the Polish star Krzysztof Martens. He is a colourful player, and he and Geir immediately found a lot of common ground in their bidding ideas. They played brilliantly together, with very little advance discussion before meeting in the playing rooms. They won easily, ahead of lots of regular, top international partnerships.

Part Three

Bidding and Conventions

Geir and Geo in Tel Aviv, receiving their trophies from Pietro Forquet

Natural talent vs artificial systems

Geir Helgemo is a player with a natural talent for bridge. He is a card player – an instinctive player – and not a theoretician. Geir likes to solve problems at the table. A tight, rigid way of playing bridge, without the opportunity for improvisation, is not a style with which he could be happy. But he has also tried that kind of bridge, at least in the bidding. Few people know that for quite a long period of his early career he played a highly artificial system. In partnership with Glenn Grøtheim he used Relay Precision, a very good system designed by Grøtheim, who has written an interesting book about it. Glenn and Geir achieved good results, and it was in this partnership that Geir made his international debut for the Norwegian open team. That was in the 1991 European Championship. With due respect to the advanced system, I think the good results came in spite of the system, and not because of it.

Also, before playing with Glenn, Geir played an artificial system with Bjørn Olav Ekren. Their relay system was in many ways based on Polish strong pass principles, although they did not actually use pass as a strong bid. The idea was to have a strong One Club opening, and a lot of relay sequences where the first answers are ambiguous and later relays clarify the ambiguity. No doubt the idea is good, at least in theory. Ekren has spoken in positive terms about it, but the truth is that he himself does not play an artificial system today.

The issue of systems and conventions is in a way a philosophical question. What should our game of bridge look like? The opponents of artificial systems number quite a few (although Harold Vanderbilt, who invented bridge in its current form, played an artificial strong club system!). The brilliant Italians' introduction of the strong, artificial One Club opening in the fifties made many important bridge personalities angry. Terence Reese´s invention, the Little Major was a reply to this, and was maybe his protest against the way bridge had developed. But the new trend in bidding was impossible to stop, even though by no means everybody liked it. I am one of those who feel happy that today natural bridge has retained its position as the way to develop the game. The majority of the world's bridge players, both at the top and the bottom, use some kind of natural system.

Some choose to compare this debate with the development of other sports, such as, for instance, the new style in ski-jumping, the skating-technique in cross-country skiing, and so on. Development never stops, you may argue, and you would normally be right. Consider the Fosbury Flop in high-jumping, for example. And the same people who, a few years ago, said ski jumping with the skis spread wide apart was an ugly look, are today delighted when they watch the fabulous Japanese skiers using an ultra-modern style of jumping. By comparison, the opponents of artificial bridge systems must from time to time admit how brilliantly the system can function when bidding various kinds of difficult hands.

Natural players should not be so inflexible that they refuse to use any systems or conventions at all. Geir Helgemo is full of respect for the bridge played in America. Due to his participation there, quite a few American conventions and styles of bidding have been adopted in Norway, but Geir once told me he does not know half of the conventions people talk about! I believe him. When playing with people in one-off partnerships, he is always trying to stop them from trying to foist their pet conventions on him!

It is possible to do very well with a natural system. But it is not a good idea to fill up the card with all kinds of conventions on top of the natural base. A large number of conventions will not help you, *per se*; it is what you use, and the structure of the whole system that matters. There is, of course, room for individual preferences. Some like particular conventions and defend their fads, arguing that they have never experienced the problems that others say can arise. All conventions have their advantages and disadvantages. What is more important is that you and your partner agree what you want to play. Arne Hofstad, the Norwegian bridge journalist, has his 'law' about this: 'It does not matter which system you play, so long as you and your partner play the same thing.'

Helgemo never wants to spend much time on the convention card. He knows about most common conventions, and he has actually published a book on the subject, but from my own experience I can tell you that he is seldom interested in discussing systems – it bores him. What is most fun in bridge is solving problems at the table. Logic, creativity and a good nose is what he needs, and has. In this way Geir is unique amongst the world's top players. Most of those players are perfectionists and you should try to emulate them. If you want to improve

Arne Hofstad

your results you should spend a lot of time preparing and training with your partner.

I will now tell you about some deals that include the bidding methods which have long been popular in Norway, and especially what I call 'Trondelag-natural', the way we bid in our area, mid-Norway (Trondelag/Trondheim). You will see that it is not only the actual conventions that are important, but also the thinking process itself. But before this, there are a couple of deals from Geir's period of artificial bidding.

As early as 1989 the 19-year-old Helgemo demonstrated the fact that even when playing an artificial system you have to use inventiveness. It is important to see all the possibilities, and it is not always enough to know all the cards partner has been dealt! You still have to use your imagination. In a knock-out match in the Norwegian Team Championship this happened:

Bjorn Olav Ekren

None Vul
Dealer S

♠ K Q 8 4 3
♡ 5
♢ A 10 7
♣ Q 7 6 5

```
      N
   W     E
      S
```

♠ A J 2
♡ A 3 2
♢ K Q J 8
♣ A 4 3

The bidding:

West	North	East	South
	Ekren		*Helgemo*
—	—	—	1♣
Pass	1NT (1)	Pass	2♣
Pass	2♠ (2)	Pass	2NT
Pass	3♢ (3)	Pass	3♡
Pass	3♠ (4)	Pass	4♣ (5)
Pass	5♣ (6)	Pass	7♢
All Pass			

This auction requires an explanation. All the bids made by South were only questions – i.e. relays – after his initial action, which showed a strong hand. South did not reveal anything about his hand, something that can be an important advantage. If the strong hand becomes declarer, the opponents do not know anything about his hand. After a natural sequence, where both players try to describe what they have, the best defence may be easier to find. But that was not the case on this deal – there was no defence at all! On the hand shown North's bidding showed the following:

(1) a singleton heart, with a positive hand (8+ HCP)
(2) spade suit (5+), and a minor side suit
(3) side suit in clubs, 5-1-3-4 or 6-1-2-4 distribution
(4) exactly 5-1-3-4, minimum (8–12 HCP)
(5) Roman Key Card Blackwood with spades as trumps
(6) 2 aces (from 5 – ♠K = an ace) plus the ♠Q

In other words, Geir knew all his partner's important cards. The conclusion, Seven Diamonds on a 4-3 fit, was pure logic. He could work out that this would be a fabulous contract. Before dummy came down the blue-print to make thirteen tricks was easy enough to work out. Two hearts had to be ruffed, and two club losers to be discarded on the spade suit. Everything would be all right as long as the side-suits did not split too badly. A heart was led, and the 4-2 split in trumps was no problem.

The young pair were, of course, satisfied with their score of 2140 on this hand, and had good hopes of picking up IMPs on the board, but it worked out even better than they had hoped! Their opponents in the other room were mere flesh and blood. They found the spade fit, investigated a bit, and concluded that a grand slam in spades was too much to hope for before they stopped in Six Spades, a reasonable contact.

But take another look at it; there are no losers outside the club suit. The fourth diamond gives a discard, but from the wrong hand, so declarer still needed to play the clubs for one loser to make his contract! As if the bridge gods wanted to make their point properly, they placed the king of clubs over the queen, and Six Spades went one down.

A few years later Glenn Grøtheim's Relay Precision was fully developed. He had worked for years perfecting it, and gave it the name the 'Viking Club'. The English version of his book should now be on the market.

Early in the eighties I was Grøtheim's partner myself. In those days the idea of using One Heart as an ambiguous response to the 'catch-all' One Diamond opening came into being. An essential principle for us was to keep the system as natural as possible, since it was already very artificial. Therefore the One Heart response was usually natural, and opener was expected to respond naturally with support. But One Heart could also be a strong hand, at least game going, with any distribution. On the next round responder could break out of the natural sequence by bidding a relay. In this way responder had two options: either to bid naturally, which was very often a good choice, or to go relaying, very often with slam ambitions. This technique was improved during the course of many of Glenn's partnerships. In the final version it became a very precise instrument.

This is what happened in another knock-out match, also in the Norwegian Championship, this time in 1991:

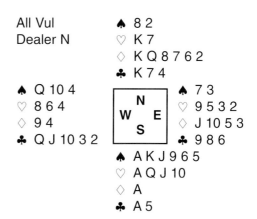

```
All Vul            ♠ 8 2
Dealer N           ♡ K 7
                   ◇ K Q 8 7 6 2
                   ♣ K 7 4
♠ Q 10 4                      ♠ 7 3
♡ 8 6 4                       ♡ 9 5 3 2
◇ 9 4                         ◇ J 10 5 3
♣ Q J 10 3 2                  ♣ 9 8 6
                   ♠ A K J 9 6 5
                   ♡ A Q J 10
                   ◇ A
                   ♣ A 5
```

The bidding:

West	North	East	South
	Grøtheim		*Helgemo*
—	1◇	Pass	1♡
Pass	2◇	Pass	2♠
Pass	2NT	Pass	3♣
Pass	3◇	Pass	3♡
Pass	3NT	Pass	4♣
Pass	4♡	Pass	4♠
Pass	4NT	Pass	5♣
Pass	5◇	Pass	7♡
All Pass			

This probably looks like Greek to you. But it is fascinating, at least when you get an explanation. Here it is:

One Heart was the two-way bid, either natural or a game-going hand. With such a strong hand it is a good idea to go into the relay structure instead of just responding One Spade, natural. Glenn (North) first bid a natural Two Diamonds, but later he just answered Geir's questions. An advantage of this method is that the questioning starts very low when using this relay, especially when opener's rebid is One Spade or One No-Trump. Sometimes a relay Roman Key Card Blackwood can be used as early as the two level, after having found partner's full distribution. In such cases the relayer can ask for high cards down to the jacks and at the end

Glenn Grøtheim

he will know just about every card in his partner's hand!

In this case, after all his questions, Geir found out that Glenn held 2-2-6-3 distribution, no aces, three kings and the queen of diamonds. Good to know, isn't it? Geir saw the golden opportunity of playing in a very unusual contract, a grand slam in hearts on a 4-2 fit, instead of an eight-card spade fit or a reasonable seven-card diamond fit.

Again, he could almost describe the play before dummy came down. And it was over in seconds. The queen of clubs was led and went to the ace. Then ace and king of spades, followed by a small spade ruffed with the king of hearts. After that came four rounds of hearts, and he could claim when trumps were 4-3.

In the other room North/South bid Seven No-Trumps, to be fair at least as good a contract. A 3-3 split in diamonds or a favourable spade split were quite good chances but, as the cards lay, the reasonable grand slam had to go down. The percentage-calculating guys can work out whether, and by how much, Seven Hearts was worse than Seven No-Trumps, but many spectators, including myself, would not have listened. We were simply enthralled to watch such a beautiful sequence, and see the spectacular contract. After the match Geir admitted he just had to try the 4-2 fit grand slam, even though from the bidding he knew Seven No-Trumps might be significantly better.

1♡/1♠ – 1NT – 2NT

After a few international events playing an artificial system Geir gave it all up. The system in his world now is, and will always be, natural. In the years that I have played with Geir we have developed our natural methods together. We agreed early on that something had to be done about the superiority of the club systems, especially when bidding big hands.

A convention we developed was the rebid of Two No-Trumps after having opened One of a major, and got the response of One No-Trump. I guess many people throughout the world use it as a forcing bid, but I think we have found a good way of using it by fitting in some hands that occasionally give natural bidders big problems. We use a standard 15–17 no-trump, so a rebid of Two No-Trumps after a One-over-One shows the 18–19 range. What about raising the One No-Trump response to Two No-Trumps?

For many years I used the bid naturally to show 18 points. That gave partner the option of passing with 6 or 7 bad points and we could avoid some shaky game contracts. To be honest, this situation rarely arose. The idea of using the Two No-Trump rebid as something else came when playing a regional team tournament in Trondheim.

```
All Vul          ♠ J 2
Dealer S         ♡ A 2
                 ◇ 10 3 2
                 ♣ K 10 8 6 5 2

            ┌─────────┐
            │    N    │
            │  W   E  │
            │    S    │
            └─────────┘

                 ♠ A K 10 9 6 5
                 ♡ 4 3
                 ◇ A 4
                 ♣ A Q 9
```

This hand is easily solved by strong club systems. But most of the players in Trondheim play natural methods, and settled for Four Spades, making eleven tricks after a heart lead. Some played in Three No-Trumps after 1♠ – 1NT – 3NT. The problem is that Seven Clubs is almost as safe as those games! It would have been easy to bring home even when West held four spades to the queen, since the queen could have been ruffed out after drawing trumps. Five spade tricks, six trump tricks (clubs) and two aces makes a total of thirteen, and the score of 2140 instead of 650. How should we have bid it?

Some people tried to argue that if South opens the bidding with Two Clubs it would at least be easy to reach slam, but South's hand is not nearly strong enough for a standard Two Club opening, is it?

The problem natural bidders have with strong, unbalanced hands after opening One of a major is substantial, especially after a One No-Trump response which can be anywhere from 6–11 HCP, and a lot of different distributions, from 3-3-3-4 to a six-card suit! Discussing this, we discovered different opinions on different bidding situations starting that way. What for instance does this mean: 1♡ – 1NT – 3◇?

Natural, of course. One-round forcing, say some; game forcing, say most. But how many diamonds are needed? Five is ideal, and then it is easier and more comfortable to bypass Three No-Trumps when responder has a slam try with diamond support. But what if the opener is 5-4 and, let's say, 19-20 HCP? Some play Two Diamonds as a one-round force over One No-Trump, and they escape with that. But as lovers of matchpoint bridge we disliked such a solution and followed traditional methods by sometimes jumping to Three Diamonds with only four diamonds. But we had to admit that such hands, and other similar hands could cause severe problems. It could be even worse for opener with 6-4 or 7-4 distribution and hands close to a Two Club opening bid.

After discussing the issue for a long time we decided to start using the Two No-Trump rebid (only over the One No-Trump response) as a game-forcing, artificial bid. What we lost was the natural, invitational sequence, and with such a hand we now have to jump to game, sometimes ending in a very shaky contract when partner holds a minimum for his One No-Trump response. Only then does the jump to game become a problem, and in some of those cases the game makes anyway. You can live with that sort of problem!

This convention solves a number of problem hands where club systems had previously been far superior. How should the weak hand respond to this Two No-Trump asking bid? It is possible to do that in different ways, but something like this sounds reasonable:

1♡	1NT	
2NT	3♣	= natural, 5 cards (+)
	3♢	= natural, 5 cards (+)
	3♡	= 3-card support
	3♠	= 2 hearts, tending to suggest 3-2-4-4
	3NT	= 5-5 in the minors

We use a four-card One Heart opening, but require five for opening One Spade. Therefore in our system there will be a slight difference between 1♡ – 1NT – 2NT and 1♠ – 1NT – 2NT. Another difference is that after 1♠ – 1NT responder may have a heart suit, but after 1♡ – 1NT he should not have a spade suit. This is how we bid after a One Spade opening:

1♠	1NT	
2NT	3♣	= unknown 5(+)-card minor
	3♢	= 4-card heart suit!
	3♡	= 5(+) cards in hearts
	3♠	= 2 spades, suggesting 2-3-4-4
	3NT	= 5-5 in the minors

Over Three Clubs, a Three Diamond bid asks which minor responder holds: Three Hearts shows a club suit, Three Spades diamonds.

The reason Three Spades shows only two spades is that we normally support immediately with three cards when the opening has guaranteed five. If you require five cards for opening One Heart as well you can amend the first scheme of responses. The Two No-Trump forcing/asking bid can be incorporated in your system whether you use four- or five-card majors, or if you use both (as we do)!

Further bidding is natural, which means this is a good way of bidding with all (very) strong, unbalanced opening hands, except the 5-5 (or 6-5) hands, which are better handled by bidding naturally. For instance, a 17–18 pointer including a good seven-card suit can be bid by saying Two No-Trumps over partner's One No-Trump response. Over responder's next bid opener simply bids his suit at the three level (or four level), and it is still possible to reach slam if the One No-Trump bidder has a maximum, including top controls.

On the above-mentioned deal from the regional match in Trondheim the superior grand slam could have been reached with the 'new' convention.

All Vul
Dealer S

♠ J 2
♡ A 2
◇ 10 3 2
♣ K 10 8 6 5 2

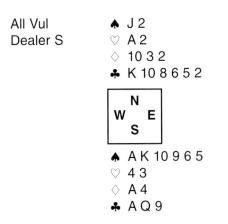

♠ A K 10 9 6 5
♡ 4 3
◇ A 4
♣ A Q 9

The bidding:

West	North	East	South
—	—	—	1♠
Pass	1NT	Pass	2NT
Pass	3♣	Pass	3◇
Pass	3♡	Pass	4♣
Pass	4♡	Pass	4NT
Pass	5♡	Pass	5NT
Pass	7♣	All Pass	

Two No-Trumps establishes the game-force, and Three Clubs promises a minor suit. Three Diamonds asks which, and Three Hearts (lowest) shows at least five clubs. Four Clubs is natural and slam invitational. Then North cue-bids the ace of hearts. Now comes Four No-Trumps, 'Roman Key Card Blackwood', and South shows two out of the five aces (the trump king included). At this stage South could gamble on the grand, but this is may be a bit too ambitious if North holds only five clubs. Five No-Trumps is a grand slam invitation, and North's sixth club enables him to accept.

Having adopted this convention, we found that the opportunity to use it came up frequently, something that proved it to be useful. There is little point to conventions that seldom or never come up – when they do either you or your partner forget it!

A couple of years after we started to use the Two No-Trump bid over partner's One No-Trump response as forcing, the convention was put to good use in TGR's Auction Pairs in London, in the summer of 1998, where I partnered Geir. In the qualifying round this hand gave us a good score:

None Vul
Dealer S

♠ A K 9 8
♡ A 10 7 6 5
◇ A
♣ A 4 2

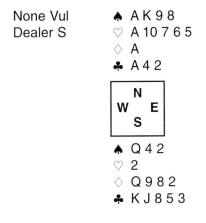

♠ Q 4 2
♡ 2
◇ Q 9 8 2
♣ K J 8 5 3

The bidding:

West	North	East	South
	Geo		*Geir*
—	—	—	Pass
Pass	1♡	Pass	1NT
Pass	2NT	Pass	3♣
Pass	4◇	Pass	4♡
Pass	6♣	All Pass	

Two No-Trumps forced to game, and Three Clubs showed a five-card suit. Later we discussed whether my Four Diamond splinter was the correct bid. There were two problems with it: first, I should really have had four-card club support, and, second, a singleton honour in the splinter suit is far from ideal. On the other hand, the good thing about bidding the splinter Four Diamonds was that I found out from my partner whether he liked his cards or not, and letting Geir Helgemo judge is seldom a bad idea!

His Four Hearts was a cue-bid and, according to our agreements, it could be a singleton. We have no way back to a heart contract in this type of sequence; that is our style, right or wrong. Over Four Hearts it was pretty obvious that Six Clubs would have chances. With a bad club suit, or a worthless diamond honour, partner would have bid Five Clubs over Four Diamonds. But he had a reasonable trump suit, the queen of spades and a heart control, so a cue-bid was reasonable

The seven of spades was led and it was up to Geir to bring home the slam. He thought for a long time before playing to the first trick. I got pretty nervous while I was waiting.

Before the lead West had produced a short, but obvious, hesitation. Geir's table feel is marvellous; he always notices such things as the time taken to make the opening lead. But here it did not determine his plan of play. He analysed the complete hand on the basis that the seven of spades was probably a doubleton.

The spade lead was taken by the ace. Then he cashed the ace of diamonds followed by a spade to the queen. A diamond was ruffed and now he played the ace of hearts and ruffed a heart. One more diamond was ruffed in dummy before he cashed the ace of clubs. The king of diamonds had not showed up, and he took another heart ruff in hand. Both defenders followed suit in hearts and diamonds. This was the ending:

So far Geir had had three chances for his contract. The king of diamonds could have dropped, if it had been in a three-card suit – but that did not happen. There was a slight chance that spades were splitting 3-3, something that Geir, as explained earlier, did not believe. Most probably East held four spades. Still there was a good chance if East also held Q-x-x in trumps. After the king of clubs declarer could simply play a spade to the king and the last spade from dummy. The jack of clubs would give him the twelfth trick en passant. None of those lines worked, but a fourth possibility came in. When the king of clubs was played, East's queen dropped. This was the full deal:

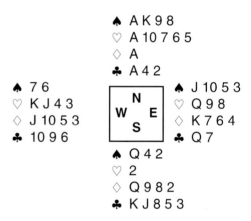

```
              ♠ A K 9 8
              ♡ A 10 7 6 5
              ◇ A
              ♣ A 4 2
♠ 7 6                         ♠ J 10 5 3
♡ K J 4 3          N          ♡ Q 9 8
◇ J 10 5 3    W       E       ◇ K 7 6 4
♣ 10 9 6          S          ♣ Q 7
              ♠ Q 4 2
              ♡ 2
              ◇ Q 9 8 2
              ♣ K J 8 5 3
```

After the king of clubs Geir simply cashed his last trump and squeezed East in spades and diamonds for the thirteenth trick.

```
              ♠ K 9
              ♡ 10 7
              ◇ —
              ♣ —
```

```
              ♠ 4
              ♡ —
              ◇ Q
              ♣ K J
```

The One Diamond response

In developing our natural bidding system we hoped to create methods to cover the most frequent problems in the bidding. We were especially keen to devise conventions to deal with the sort of situations where artificial club systems had shown themselves superior. The above-mentioned Two No-Trump rebid after the response of One No-Trump was just such a solution. Another idea was to use an initial One Diamond response to a One Club opening to be flexible. Most of us decided to use the response as either natural and weak (normally a six-card suit), or as a game-going hand either with diamonds and a major, or club support. Some of us also like to use 1◇ – 2♣ as consistent with a strong hand with support for opener's suit. These methods mean that you do not have to play inverted minor-suit raises, although many people are happy to do so.

The real advantage lies in the efficiency of the One Diamond response. By using it as weak with long diamonds, or as a game-going hand, we can keep the bidding low in situations where slam prospects needed to be investigated.

Opener	Responder
1♣	1◇
1♡	2♣

Two Clubs in this situation can now become a slam invitation with a club fit, though normally only three-card support (with club support and a weak hand we support at once and do not introduce the diamonds). This means the Two Club rebid would also have been a slam try if opener's second bid had been One Spade or One No-Trump. In these positions Three Clubs would indicate a stronger slam try, with at least four-card support

Tor Helness

Opener	Responder
1♣	1◇
1♡	2♡

Two Hearts shows a slam try with a diamond suit and four-card heart support. With a weaker diamond/heart hand responder would skip the diamonds and bid his hearts at once, even if he had longer diamonds. The advantage of doing things this way is, of course, that you keep the bidding low and get efficient auctions when you have strong hands. The disadvantage is that you may have problems getting to the best partscore when your side has a diamond fit, though what comes back as partial compensation is that the defence is tougher when responder conceals his diamond suit.

A memorable hand was this one from a knock-out match in Norway in 1994. It was the last match before the play-off, and the Students Bridgeclub from Trondheim met Carnegie from Oslo.

NS Vul   ♠ A 8 3
Dealer N   ♡ K 7
                ◇ Q 8 2
                ♣ A J 8 6 3

♠ 9 7 5 4   ♠ K Q 10 6
♡ Q 10 9 5   N   ♡ 8 6 4 2
◇ J 6 5 4   W   E   ◇ 10
♣ 10   S   ♣ 9 7 5 2

                ♠ J 2
                ♡ A J 3
                ◇ A K 9 7 3
                ♣ K Q 4

The bidding:

Closed Room:

West	North	East	South
	Løwe		Helness
—	1♣	Pass	2◇
Pass	3◇	Pass	4NT
Pass	5♠	Pass	7◇
All Pass			

By the way, it is worth noting that one of the players in the Oslo team was Tor Helness, so there was considerably more at stake than simply winning or losing!

The Oslo pair had a practical sequence to end up in a reasonable

Per Løwe

grand slam. A spade was led and Helness immediately played two rounds of trumps. The bad diamond split doomed the contract, and since declarer could not get the clubs going quickly enough to pitch his spade loser, the defence soon claimed two down, for 200 to the Students Bridgeclub.

In the Open Room the bidding went:

West	North	East	South
	Helgemo		Ekren
—	1♣	Pass	1◇
Pass	1NT	Pass	2♣
Pass	3♣	Pass	3◇
Pass	3♡	Pass	4◇
Pass	4NT	Pass	5♣
Pass	7NT	All Pass	

Of course, there was an unfortunate trump break for the Oslo pair in the Closed Room but Seven No-Trumps is a much better contract. The bidding to the superior grand slam was beautifully controlled. Ekren's slam try (Two Clubs) was at an economically low level, and Three Clubs from North indicated some interest and suggested a fifth club. The continuation was an exchange of cue-bids followed by Roman Key Card Blackwood.

The king of spades was led to the ace. In Seven No-Trumps Geir could test the clubs first, and the bad split in that suit suggested to declarer that a bad diamond break was not unlikely. Geir read the distribution correctly and played the eight of diamonds, which collected the ten and dummy's ace. Then Geir calmly ran the seven of diamonds – always a significant card for Scandinavians (and in some places in the UK), as it is the beer-card – everyone has to buy you a drink if you manage to take the last trick with it. Thirteen tricks meant 20 IMPs to the young players from Trondheim, and the veterans from Oslo were beaten by a very small margin, 99-96!

Psyching

Some of you may believe that Geir Helgemo psychs frequently. You may have read bridge columns and magazines detailing situations where people have been totally fooled by such bids. But, in fact, that is seldom the case, and far from an everyday happening. If the cards run quiet, Geir can play steadily for hours without doing anything out of the ordinary. And that is a strategy which has a lot to recommend it. To try to create something out of nothing all the time is not a winning policy. But, when the opportunity arises, he will strike while the iron is hot. Even so, there are many excellent ways of getting good results without psyching.

So, in Helgemo's world of bridge the psychic bid is not a significant element. But when the opportunity arises we can admire Geir for his ability to make the unusual bid at just the right time. The poker element in bridge is exactly the same as in poker itself: you must be able to afford the potential loss if you are going to win by bluffing. Here is an exciting example from an international junior event:

EW Vul
Dealer N

♠ K 10 7 6 4
♡ K Q 8 3
◇ —
♣ K 9 4 3

♠ A 3　　　　　　♠ Q J 2
♡ A 6 4　　　　　♡ J 10 5
◇ K 10 5 4　　　◇ A Q 9 7 6 3
♣ A Q 10 8　　　♣ 2

♠ 9 8 5
♡ 9 7 2
◇ J 8 2
♣ J 7 6 5

The bidding:

West	North	East	South
			Geir
—	1♠	Pass	2♡ (!)
Pass	4◇ (1)	Pass	4♡
All Pass			

(1) cue-bid, heart support

East paused briefly before passing over North's One Spade opening, which inspired Geir to psych. This deal took place in Geir's junior period. There was a risk of course: he might have talked East/West out of a failing slam. A bigger danger for Geir was that the cards could have been placed in such a way that his opponents could have doubled the final contract. But who doubles a game contract after the opponents have gone through a cue-bidding sequence?

Another risk for the psycher is that partner drives to a slam! However, in this case both Geir's partner and East/West were fooled. Some would say that East should have bid Two Diamonds on the first round, and others might say that West should have doubled Four Hearts. Well, maybe, but they were both pretty sure their partner had nothing. In the end they could only collect three undoubled undertricks for 150.

In the other room Geir's team-mates played a dull Three No-Trumps for 660. Good luck you may say, but, once East had failed to bid Two Diamonds, who was in command at the table?

Creativity

In 1996 the Norwegian national team was invited to the bridge festival in Tel Aviv. At the time two-thirds of Norway's team played at the Nidaros Bridge Club in Trondheim. The four were Glenn Grøtheim with Terje Aa and Tor Helness in partnership with Helgemo. The Norwegian Bridge Federation decided that they should compete in Tel Aviv, but unfortunately for the team Tor Helness was unable to go. That was lucky for me, because I was called upon as a substitute. Geir and I played a lot together in national events in Norway from 1995–98, so we could go to Israel at short notice without feeling totally unprepared.

It was a fantastic trip and, although I cannot prove it, I feel sure Geir played as well there as he has ever done. After more than 300 deals, I could find only one mistake and he made that when declaring a partscore contract. Otherwise he played completely error-free bridge, and produced a number of sensational hands to bring in the points from all directions. I played my normal game – which meant at least a couple of mistakes in every session – but that was more than enough for us to finish on top in most of the events we played. What I remember most clearly from the week in Tel Aviv is Geir's play of a slam (see page 91), and a bidding sequence demonstrating his flair for creative bidding.

Our partnership uses a Two No-Trump response over a major-suit opening as a game-forcing bid with at least four-card support (Jacoby-style). After the Two No-Trump response both opener and responder have the opportunity to choose between cue-bidding and asking bids to discover partner's short suit. In the open pairs Geir used this convention but in a very imaginative fashion. I held this hand:

♠ 7 3 2
♥ A 10 9 8 7
♦ K 9 8
♣ A 2

It was just enough for a minimum One Heart opening and Geir made the above-mentioned Two No-Trump response. My Three Hearts showed a minimum, at which point Geir could have asked me to cue-bid by bidding Three No-Trumps, but instead he said Three Spades, showing a singleton himself. He had slam interest despite my showing a minimum, so I had to re-examine my hand in a different light. And to be honest, it would be hard to envisage a much better fitting hand than opener's 11-pointer. All the cards were working well, and nothing was wasted in spades. In addition, my heart suit was a five-carder (we used four-card major openings) with good fillers, to boot. There was no reason to complicate matters, so I jumped to Four No-Trumps, Roman Key Card Blackwood. Both Geir's hand and his response to my Blackwood enquiry were unusual:

None Vul   ♠ 7 3 2
Dealer N   ♥ A 10 9 8 7
            ♦ K 9 8
            ♣ A 2

```
        N
    W       E
        S
```

♠ A Q
♥ Q J 6 5
♦ A Q 10 7 3
♣ K 3

The bidding:

West	North	East	South
	Geo		*Geir*
—	1♡	Pass	2NT
Pass	3♡	Pass	3♠ (!)
Pass	4NT	Pass	6NT (!)
All Pass			

Geir had no real intention of stopping below slam whatever I did, but his Three Spade bid was rather creative – showing a singleton with ace-queen doubleton does not constitute everyday bidding! And why? There were two reasons – the first being that this might provoke a double, which would let him know that the finesse was losing. But additionally his bid got the reaction he wanted. For one thing, if opener has a minimum but still jumps directly from Three Spades to Blackwood he must have something special, must he not? To have a reason to make such a bid, I simply had to have both the missing honours in the side suits. If I controlled only one of them I would have made a cue-bid, and with a singleton and a nice minimum hand (5-4-3-1 distribution), I was systemically allowed to show it directly over Two No-Trumps as if I had extras. So I could not have that sort of hand, and Geir could read my actual hand-type like an open book. Six No-Trumps had to be the right spot, and so indeed it proved, whatever the scoring. Six No-Trumps gave us close to a clear top, since there was nothing to the play when diamonds behaved normally.

During that bridge week in Israel we played three main tournaments and some minor events. After the last session of the open pairs we were pretty sure we had won. Our estimates gave us 65% for the session. That meant the Polish pair closest to us needed more than 70% to beat us.

When the results first came on the screen we were terribly disappointed. Next to our names there stood a score of 60.5% and the Poles were celebrating since they had scored 67% in the last session. We simply could not believe it.

We sat down to play the next tournament – a less important side-event – quite depressed. But we really could not give up on the idea that there had been a scoring error. While playing the side-event I managed to become dummy fairly often and thus had the chance to investigate the results in the chaotic scoring room. To get access to any of the results was far from easy; if you ever want to try it, remember to fill in the complaint form in Hebrew!

By enlisting the help of a young local fan – a boy who had kibitzed the famous Helgemo for the whole week – the search finally produced results, and at last we found the mistake. We had played Three No-Trumps making two overtricks on a combined 32 HCP where there were all sorts of bad breaks: a good result. Almost the whole field had climbed to the slam and gone one or more down. The problem was that our 660 was entered on the wrong side of the score sheet! We had got a complete zero on the board instead of a shared top! Our score in the last session had to be corrected to 64.8 %, and first place in the event was restored to Norway.

On returning to the table where Geir was trying to play bridge for both of us, I kept the good news to myself for a while. But when I jumped up to buy us both a well-deserved beer, he was tired of seeing me leave the table all the time, and he said: 'Here I am trying to win this tournament, while you are still trying to win the last one.'

The next hand occurred in a regional championship. Geir was dealt this hand as North with no-one vulnerable:

♠ A J 2
♡ Q J 7
◇ A J 4
♣ A K Q 6

The bidding:

West	North	East	South
—	2NT	Pass	3◇ (1)
Pass	3♡	Pass	4♣ (2)
Pass	4◇ (3)	Pass	4NT
Pass	?		

(1) transfer to hearts
(2) natural, slam-try
(3) cue-bid, agreeing hearts

In fact, hearts were established as trumps at this stage, and Four No-Trumps was Roman Key Card Blackwood. What do you think Geir responded?

No, he didn't show his three aces. He bid Seven Clubs! That ended the auction, and these were the North/South cards:

None Vul
Dealer N

♠ A J 2
♡ Q J 7
◇ A J 4
♣ A K Q 6

♠ 10 9
♡ A K 10 8 2
◇ K 3
♣ J 5 4 2

Most people would be happy to bid a slam on these cards, but the grand slam in clubs is as good as lay-down. How could Helgemo bid it this way?

Geir had all the three top clubs, and since he was partnering a good player he could trust South to have something special as he had neither made a cue-bid nor signed off after having made his slam try. South's bidding had to be based on the ace-king of hearts and an outside king, or on the ace-king of hearts and a five-card club suit. In either case Seven Clubs is the superior contract. If South holds only one heart honour it is difficult to think of any hand that would qualify for the Four No-Trump bid, when looking at North's cards. Seven Clubs will normally make even if both clubs and hearts are breaking badly, just by taking a diamond ruff in the South hand. Five hearts, five club tricks, the ace of spades and the two top tricks in diamonds make a total of thirteen. The play turned out to be a formality.

Logic

Fine conventions on your card can never act as a replacement for pure logic. If you can combine a simple system with good judgement, and maybe a dash of creativity, you will have the winning formula.

When they played the Macallan Invitational in London in January 1999, Helness and Helgemo crushed the field for the second year in a row. Tor and Geir play a simple system, but compensate with a remarkable understanding of the game.

This hand provides the proof:

None Vul
Dealer S

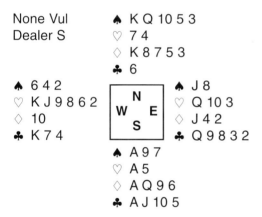

was a cue-bid, allowing Roman Key Card Blackwood with diamonds agreed as trumps. Geir showed one ace (the king of diamonds) and Tor's Five No-Trump continuation told his partner that their side held all the aces (including the trump king) and the trump queen. Geir concluded reasonably that Seven Diamonds should be the final contract. He knew that the thirteenth trick would come from a heart ruff in the short hand. South had shown four clubs (from the opening bid) and four-card diamond support, which left him with at most five major cards.

Not impressed? Well, it may not appear so scientific, but in a logical way they had bid a laydown grand slam with only 27 HCP. The expert field had problems duplicating the result – only one other pair in the field managed the feat.

The bidding:

West	North	East	South
	Helgemo		Helness
—	—	—	1♣
1♡	1♠	Pass	2NT
Pass	3♢	Pass	4♢
Pass	4♠	Pass	4NT
Pass	5♢	Pass	5NT
Pass	7♢	All Pass	

This was natural bidding at its best. The key bid in this case was perhaps Helness' Four Diamond raise. This made it a lot easier to find the top spot because he concealed his spade support. Four Spades

Out of the frying pan

There is an old rule to the effect that you should not try to rescue your partner when he has overcalled and been doubled. Players are taught not to bid their own suit, but to leave partner to play the hand. The idea is to trust partner to have what he has promised, in which case trying to rescue him would lead to an even worse result. That is how the experts used to reason, and that is what many still believe.

But in modern bridge the overcalling style has changed significantly. Nowadays people make overcalls with minimal HCP, and even with remarkably feeble suits! This is standard strategy for many players, especially on distributional hands. It is certainly possible to miss your own top spot by being too passive and passing because the suit is not good enough for an old-fashioned overcall. Today, this danger is considered more serious according to many players than, for instance, the possibility that your partner may lead unsuccessfully from his king-doubleton, or that your overcall gets heavily penalised. Let us say you are dealt this hand as North:

♠ J 10 9 7 5
♡ 2
♢ A Q 10 9
♣ Q 10 2

West deals and bid One Club. Many players are reluctant to bid One Spade because of the weak suit. From time to time you hear suggestions that you might bid One Diamond instead! I think they worry too much about partner's lead, and forget that their own side may be able to declare the hand. Let us say partner holds:

Zia Mahmood

♠ A 6 5 3 2
♡ 10 9 7 4
♢ 4 3
♣ K 6

If North passes and East, for instance, bids Three Clubs, North/South are in trouble. It is much more dangerous to come in now, and very often East/West will be left to play happily in their partscore. As you can see, Four Spades is a good spot for North/South, and normally the contract will come home with a diamond finesse through the opener, clearly an inviting prospect.

A more offensive style of overcalling and opening bids leads to a greater danger of being penalised. Also, aggressive pre-emptive openings are popular, for instance, at the two and three level. The old rule of trusting partner on such occasions therefore perhaps needs revising. Helgemo had the guts to say it out loud: 'You simply use the old rule, but change one word,' he once said to me, of course partly in jest. Instead of 'Never try to rescue your partner' it should read 'Always try to rescue your partner'. This was, of course, a joke, but there is some truth in it as well. Especially when playing matchpoints, one can from time to time be pretty sure that partner is about to be taken to the cleaners. The attempt to rescue partner may be a failure, but very often there is a better spot available somewhere – and if you do not try to find it you will be doomed anyway.

Through his many international games Geir Helgemo has had many clashes with Zia Mahmood. They are good friends, but it is especially enjoyable to beat up your friends, is it not? I am sure they will not mind my telling this story to illustrate our theme. In the 1998 Macallan tournament Zia and Andy Robson were soundly beaten by Helgemo and Helness. This hand from that event did not go well for Zia:

The bidding:

West	North	East	South
Geir	*Andrew*	*Tor*	*Zia*
—	—	—	1NT
Dble	All Pass		

It is popular these days to open One No-Trump with hands that include five-card major suits. It can lead to missing partscores on 5-3 major suit fits, but there are compensating advantages in showing a balanced hand immediately.

However, on this deal Zia's One No-Trump opening ended up as a spectacular disaster. Perhaps Robson should have run to Two Clubs, or Zia should have escaped from the doubled contract, but have some sympathy with them. Besides: real men do not rescue themselves! And again, how often has a long suit, like Zia's spades in this instance, been what helped a doubled no-trump contract to make?

Against One No-Trump doubled Geir took his six diamond tricks. Tor discarded three spades and two clubs. Geir saw he probably had to cash his club trick while he was still on lead, and he duly did so. Tor threw his last spade away now and took the rest of the tricks with his hearts when Geir switched to that suit.

One of the world's greatest card players – the popular Zia – had just played in One No-Trump doubled making zero tricks! Seven down doubled gives the unusual score of 2000 – yes, it is a score as well as a year! Unfortunately, I was not there when this happened, but I am sure Tor and Geir did not gloat over the result. On the other hand, I am sure Andy and Zia would have given the kibitzers a rueful smile. But their nightmare was not yet over…

All Vul
Dealer S

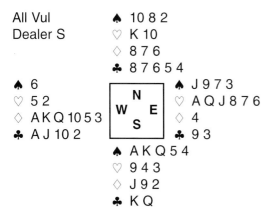

♠ 10 8 2
♡ K 10
◇ 8 7 6
♣ 8 7 6 5 4

♠ 6
♡ 5 2
◇ A K Q 10 5 3
♣ A J 10 2

♠ J 9 7 3
♡ A Q J 8 7 6
◇ 4
♣ 9 3

♠ A K Q 5 4
♡ 9 4 3
◇ J 9 2
♣ K Q

Rescue your man

...Going for a penalty of 2000 can be quite soul-destroying. In a match where you begin with 30-30 (VPs) but can end up with 0-60 if you lose 30 IMPs, you are in real trouble when you have this sort of disaster. Playing matchpoints you might get back a stone-cold bottom by making an overtrick in a partscore – but not here. Nevertheless, in this case Zia and Robson had more boards to play against the Vikings before getting away from them, so they had to find a way to even the score. On the next board Helgemo, South, held:

♠ 8 4
♡ 6
♢ Q J 7 6 5 3
♣ 10 9 7 3

South had dealt and no one was vulnerable. Robson opened in second seat with One Spade and Helness overcalled Two Hearts. After two passes Robson re-

Andrew Robson

opened with a double. Both Helness and Zia passed, and it was Geir's turn. I think few players would have even thought of bidding. But Geir felt that his partner was about to score very badly and although his decision to bid Three Diamonds might not receive the *Good Housekeeping* seal of approval, you might say that about the final result as well. This was the full hand:

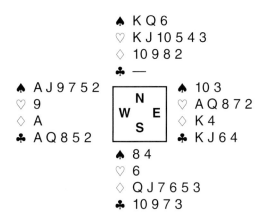

♠ K Q 6
♡ K J 10 5 4 3
♢ 10 9 8 2
♣ —

♠ A J 9 7 5 2   ♠ 10 3
♡ 9   ♡ A Q 8 7 2
♢ A   ♢ K 4
♣ A Q 8 5 2   ♣ K J 6 4

♠ 8 4
♡ 6
♢ Q J 7 6 5 3
♣ 10 9 7 3

What a dummy! Three Diamonds was also doubled, and Geir was not sure whether he was awake or dreaming when Tor put down his hand. East and West's judgement to defend here could certainly be questioned, but the state of the match obviously had something to do with it. Three Diamonds doubled made nine tricks for plus 470 to North/South. As you can see, East/West have an easy game in spades, and it is also possible to make a club slam if you play the hand carefully. (The play in Six Clubs by West on a diamond lead is interesting. You must cash the king of clubs rather than leading out the ace or queen. Then you can ruff a spade high in dummy and finesse twice in trumps.) But regardless of that, you can at least see that it sometimes pays to rescue partner!

Part Four

Laugh and the World Laughs With You

Who are the fools?

Most parts of this book express my, and other people's, admiration for Helgemo's special bridge talent. As well as possessing remarkable qualities, he has also worked hard to make the most of them. However, luckily he is no computer. And anyone of flesh and blood who needs to solve problems for which there is no hundred percent solution will fail from time to time. Even Homer nods, and even Geir Helgemo fails!

When the idea for this book first came up, we discussed how to put it together, agreeing to make chapters with themes such as declarer play, defence, and bidding, and so on, instead of arranging the material chronologically. I wanted a chapter containing mistakes and near misses. Geir has an excellent sense of humour as well as a good self-deprecating wit, and when the suggestion for such a chapter came up he agreed immediately. I am not sure all of the world's bridge superstars would have done so. But he also said with a smile: 'I certainly hope that it will be a short chapter.'

While I thought he would be right, I soon found lots of stories in direct contrast to all the wonderful bridge in Helgemo's world, though there are very few boards where Geir made clear-cut errors.

When he was helping me with the text for this book Geir and I played in a local tournament in Trøndelag. With Geir as partner it would have been a minor disaster not to end up in the top placings, but that day everything went wrong. Of course, things do not work out well every time we play, but on this particular Saturday I could feel that my partner was playing at least as badly as I. Nothing was working, and we went from table to table getting killed by everyone.

For example, on the very first board of the tournament Geir found the expert lead of the ace of hearts from A-Q-x against a Four Spade contract on a deal where it sounded as if the opponents had a long running club suit ready for discards. I have seen him find leads like that many times, and I have often wondered how he does it. But this time, the lead was a catastrophe. Declarer made two extra tricks because of the lead, and our result, minus 650, found its lonely place at the bottom of the score sheet.

A couple of rounds were played without any further catastrophes. Then Geir became declarer in Four Spades.

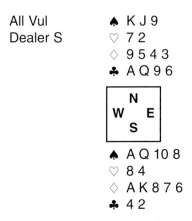

```
All Vul          ♠ K J 9
Dealer S         ♡ 7 2
                 ◇ 9 5 4 3
                 ♣ A Q 9 6

                     N
                 W       E
                     S

                 ♠ A Q 10 8
                 ♡ 8 4
                 ◇ A K 8 7 6
                 ♣ 4 2
```

The bidding:

West	North	East	South
	Geo		*Geir*
—	—	—	1◇
3♡	Dble	Pass	4♠
All Pass			

The double of Three Hearts was negative, normally showing a four-card spade suit. I took a chance by doubling with only three cards in the suit because of my high-card values and excellent diamond support.

In a similar situation playing in the European Championship Pairs in The Hague a negative double with three cards in the unbid major went totally wrong. Geir had no stopper in the opponent's suit and king-queen doubleton in the other major. His fertile imagination came up with the idea of finding a perfect fit, which would have led us to the superior contract of K-Q facing A-J-10-x! Four Hearts could have been a remarkable contract, but since I had only A-J-x we were the only pair in the tournament who deliberately played in a major-suit game with a 3-2 fit. Understandably, I should say. He was searching for a 4-2 fit, I for a 4-3 fit, so it was not so surprising that we were short of a couple of trumps....

Anyway, this time the negative double led to an excellent contract. West led the ace and king of hearts before switching to the three of clubs. If the king of clubs was onside the game contract could be made, even against a 3-1 split in diamonds. But there was a big danger of a club ruff if West held a singleton club. So Geir put up the ace of clubs, and then the contract seemed to depend on the 2-2 split in diamonds, did it not?

In theory that is the only chance, but for Geir the concept of 'the only chance' does not exist. After the ace of clubs, Geir called for the nine of diamonds from dummy. East covered with the jack and the ace of diamonds took the trick. When the ten of diamonds fell from West's hand, I began to like the situation. Geir thought for a while and then played three rounds of spades ending in dummy. The trumps were 3-3, and next he played a diamond towards his hand. East, a young and inexperienced player, followed with the two.

This position is what the world calls an idiot's finesse. If East was originally dealt Q-J-2 and West the singleton ten, the defence had started life with a sure trick. In

that case East's sacrifice of the jack would have been a terrible misplay. So in other words South should not take the finesse, in theory. But in practice the position is less clear-cut. Poor players often make this sort of mistake. In any event that was what happened this sad Saturday. Geir took the finesse in diamonds, and this was the complete hand:

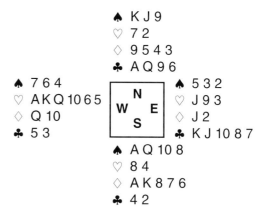

A score close to a top had been transformed into a shared bottom. Four Spades was cold as the cards lay, but Five Diamonds would have been beaten because the club finesse loses. I could do nothing but laugh, and I must admit the only thing which could have made me laugh more would have been if the king of clubs was onside. If so, the genius would have gone down when everyone else would have taken eleven tricks in as many seconds.

I will spare you the details of the rest of this tournament. But I can tell you that some rounds after this Four Spade contract, I could no longer keep quiet. I said, loudly enough that some of the closest tables could hear me: 'It is only just past eleven o'clock in the morning, but if things continue like this we will be done with that chapter on mistakes before lunch.'

The response came quickly from the other side of the table. 'Yes, and we will soon have enough for a second book too.'

Courage or arrogance?

To play for a lie of the cards that means the opponents have done something very foolish could be perceived as a bit arrogant. But if they have perpetrated a huge mistake it feels wrong not to try to take advantage of it. Even so, it takes courage to take a finesse as Geir did on the previous hand. When it goes wrong he has made a fool of himself, particularly since he is such a big star. I laughed at him, but to be honest, I am quite sure that when he takes chances like that it brings in more points than it loses.

In a play-off match in the Norwegian Teams Championship everybody got the chance to laugh at Norway's best player:

None Vul   ♠ A K J 4 2
Dealer E   ♡ A Q 6 5
              ◇ 6 2
              ♣ Q 6

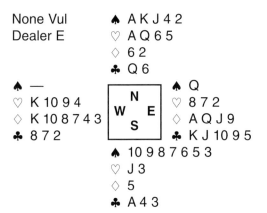

♠ —   ♠ Q
♡ K 10 9 4   ♡ 8 7 2
◇ K 10 8 7 4 3   ◇ A Q J 9
♣ 8 7 2   ♣ K J 10 9 5

              ♠ 10 9 8 7 6 5 3
              ♡ J 3
              ◇ 5
              ♣ A 4 3

The East/West contract of Five Diamonds went one down in the Closed Room. In the Open Room East/West also pushed all the way to Five Diamonds, but Geir's partner drove him to Five Spades. As you can see, the contract is safe as long as the king of hearts is onside for declarer, but Geir did not know that this was the case, and he is always on the look-out for additional chances.

West led a club to the queen, king and ace. Geir drew trumps and then took a couple of extra round of trumps just to see if something happened – and it did! East discarded an encouraging eight of hearts. Since he had opened the bidding, Geir decided to play him for the king of hearts.

In an attempt to fool his opponents, Geir played a heart to the ace and another heart from dummy towards his jack. Of course, this risks looking silly, especially when the king is onside, but every time East holds the king this is the best option.

Some would say this play was hopeless because East will always put up his king. After all, he can count the number of hearts in the South hand if the defence use count signals. But this kind of deceptive play has succeeded many times. East will very often think along the following lines: 'It is not possible that declarer would play like this if his contract depended on the simple heart finesse.' Sometimes, he will conclude that his partner's carding was wrong (or that he had not bothered to signal at all) and that declarer had started life with a singleton, so he will play low.

Of course, when this hand was played, East did indeed play low, since he had nothing else to do. West scored his unexpected heart trick, and one trick in each minor suit plus the king of hearts defeated the laydown contract. I was not there when this happened, unfortunately, but I am told later that Mr Helgemo turned a bright shade of red immediately afterwards.

System discussion

It was not difficult to get details about the previous hand. Bjørn Olav (Boek) Ekren was Geir's partner when the hand was played, and he was more than happy to give me the details. Bjørn Olav has a high respect for Helgemo's abilities, but this hand represented perhaps the most embarrassing incident in Geir's career to date. It was even reported in a newspaper column and got a special place in his clippings collection.

Boek Ekren himself has gone far in Norwegian bridge. He has been a top player at national level for years, but his invention, Ekren's Two Diamond opening, is probably his greatest claim to fame. The convention became very popular in Norway as soon as it was invented. Before that, a few players from Trondheim, including myself, used a weak Flannery Two Diamond opening, showing four spades and five hearts and 10–12 HCP. Boek went further and soon an extreme version of the Two Diamond opening was in use. More recently, it has been referred to as 'the Norwegian Two Diamonds'. I do not know if I should be proud or ashamed.

In the beginning we played the convention with enthusiasm and when we discovered the havoc this opening caused, we were sure this was the way forward. Soon we opened Two Diamonds with anything, even if we were only 4-4 in the majors. The most extreme hand I opened Two Diamonds on was this one:

♠ 9 8 3 2
♡ 8 7 4 3
♢ 10 2
♣ 9 7

Yes, you are right, the hand has only twelve cards. But in my eagerness to open with this new super convention I did not notice that! After all, I did have two doubletons! My excuse is that the hand was played late in the evening on a very festive occasion, a rubber game on a friend's 35th birthday. After I had been doubled in some horrible contract and a few cards had been played, it was clear I was heading towards an inevitable 1100 down. Then I discovered that I was a card short and tried to get the deal cancelled. But no, my opponents refused to let me off and insisted on their 1100. My only consolation was that it would have been 1400 if I had had the four of clubs which we found under the table a while later.

Despite its obvious weaknesses, some people still play 'the Norwegian Two Diamonds'. It is a difficult convention to defend against, especially when responder has some support for at least one of the majors. Some people open Two Hearts to show a weak hand with both majors. That has some advantages (the next hand does not have a 'free' double) but it is much more dangerous. One of the good things about Boek's Two Diamonds is that it is possible for the auction to 'die' in Two Diamonds if responder has a long diamond suit, and that is not possible if you open Two Hearts.

Most of the top players in Trondheim used this Two Diamond opening. I remember Helgemo once said, 'It is always the right thing to do when you have both majors and a weak hand.' But this was when he was still a junior. We soon discovered that the word 'always' had to be amended to 'sometimes'. The convention produced swings, but all too often they were the swings in the wrong direction. Then people began to insist that the opening needed at least 5-4 in the majors, and that the bid had to be used with discretion. Consequently, the frequency of the opening was reduced, and the players' enthusiasm for it decreased accordingly. Today, only a few pairs still have the convention on their system card. Even Bjørn Olav Ekren does not now play his own convention!

Norway's 'flagship' in international bridge has for many years been the partnership of Tor Helness and Geir Helgemo. For a long time they played the Norwegian 'Two Diamonds', in spite of the fact that Geir's enthusiasm for the convention had become very low. The reason they took so long to discard it was probably inertia.

In early 1999 Geir and Tor played in the Cap Gemini in the Netherlands, and were still using the convention. Geir and Tor live a long way apart, Geir in Trondheim and Tor 500km away in Oslo. The following week they had their usual system discussion – in an aeroplane, from when they sat down in their seats to the moment when the stewardess arrived with refreshments. Flying to London to play the Macallan and defend their triumph from the previous year, Geir told

Tor that they had to remove the Norwegian Two Diamonds from the system card. Tor wanted to know why. Well, the Macallan Tournament allows simple systems only and to the best of Geir's knowledge the convention was prohibited in that tournament. Then refreshments came, and the system discussion was over! Tor gave in, and a standard weak Two Diamonds was inscribed on their system card for the first time.

In Round 2 of the tournament they met a pair playing Two Diamonds as weak with both majors. Tor wondered if they were allowed to do that, but it was confirmed that there was no problem. Geir looked a little shame-faced. But, as he said, once they had inscribed the weak Two on their system card, it would not be a good omen to change in the middle of a tournament! That was that. With or without the help of the weak Two Diamonds they won the Macallan for the second year in a row.

This story helps proves that Arne Hofstad's law of systems still holds good: it does not matter which system you play, as long as it is the same one as your partner!

Schadenfreude

When the best players do well everyone looks at them with respect, and is proud to know them. But when they do not succeed, the air can suddenly fill with *schadenfreude*, i.e. pleasure derived from the discomfort of others. The gossip spreads through the playing area, and soon everybody knows what error the superstar made. When the expert plays in a very clever way and the cards fail to cooperate, it can be extremely funny. However, in truth there is often good reason to feel sorry for the expert who tries something imaginative that fails.

In the 1996 European Pairs Championship I felt sorry for Geir on this deal. Not only did it cost him a bushel of matchpoints, but also a large number of Swiss francs, since the incident occurred in the final, and of course it affected the prize money we received. He played the hand well, after I had taken a bit of a shot in the bidding:

All Vul
Dealer S

```
              ♠ 8 7 6 4
              ♡ 2
              ◇ 7 6
              ♣ Q J 10 7 3 2
           ┌───────────┐
           │     N     │
           │ W       E │
           │     S     │
           └───────────┘
              ♠ A J 9
              ♡ Q 10 9 4
              ◇ A K Q 2
              ♣ A 6
```

The bidding:

West	North	East	South
—	—	—	2NT
Pass	3♣	Pass	3◇
Pass	3♡	Pass	3NT
All Pass			

Holding the North cards it was difficult to know what to do over partner's Two No-Trump opening. I chose 'Puppet Stayman'. After all, opener could hold a five-card spade suit, and if so game in spades could be cold. Things might work out even if South had only a four-card spade suit. But on this occasion of course, he could not help me with spades at all. Three Diamonds showed at least one four-card major, and my Three Hearts suggested spades. Three No-Trumps from South indicated that there was no fit, but as an optimistic guy I still had some hopes of success. Maybe partner would be able to run the club suit.

West knew about South's heart suit and led the ten of spades. East produced the queen and Geir the ace. Declarer continued with the jack of spades and West surprisingly showed out, discarding the three of hearts, an encouraging card. East took the trick with the king of spades and obediently switched to the jack of hearts. South's queen was covered by the king; then West played the five of hearts, East produced the seven and South won with his ten. Geir cashed his nine of spades and West threw a diamond. Now Geir cashed his three top diamonds and West, who had originally held three diamonds, got rid of a club. Now the hand was as an open book for a player of Geir's ability. The end-position presumably looked like this:

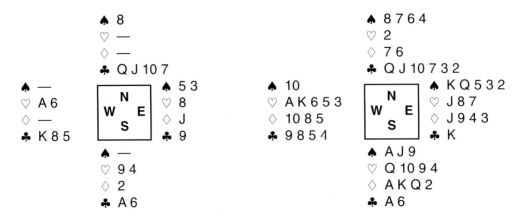

The location of the heart honours was known and it was not unreasonable for West to try a small heart on the second round of the suit. After all East could have been dealt the ten of hearts. The full distribution was also known.

West could be thrown in with a heart and could make two tricks in the suit, but then he would have to lead a club, which would hand declarer an entry to dummy where he could collect the eight of spades, declarer's ninth trick.

To be sure of endplaying West in the diagrammed situation Geir played the nine of hearts from hand, a careful play. West took his two hearts and then came the expected club switch. The contract was duly made, and I expected something close to a top. However, one thing spoiled the party. The full deal actually looked like this:

Geir had nearly worked out the opponents' cards perfectly. Only two cards had switched places, the king and nine of clubs. Geir's endplay worked well, and with three cards left he made the rest. The 'mistake' was that East held the singleton king of clubs all the time, and less inspired players than Geir made ten or eleven tricks, by plonking the ace of clubs on the table early in the play. They collected six tricks in the suit and had an easy time of it.

At our table the defender holding the singleton king was clearly satisfied. It looked as if he felt that he had fooled the Great Helgemo. We found some consolation in the fact that we scored an average on the board anyway, due to the fact that quite a few pairs did not bid the game. But if the king of clubs had been with West the result would surely have been rather different.

A bad hand – what's that?

During the nineties Trondheim was normally represented by two teams in Norway's Premier League, which meant many matches with more issues at stake than just the result. The players knew each other very well from several clashes in regional matches, and often played against friends who had been partners or team-mates the previous year. In one of these matches Geir showed the true extent of his creativity:

```
None Vul        ♠ K Q 4
Dealer N        ♡ 9
                ◇ J 9 2
                ♣ A K J 10 9 8
```

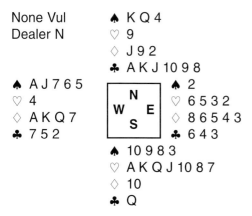

```
♠ A J 7 6 5          ♠ 2
♡ 4             N    ♡ 6 5 3 2
◇ A K Q 7    W   E   ◇ 8 6 5 4 3
♣ 7 5 2         S    ♣ 6 4 3
```

```
                ♠ 10 9 8 3
                ♡ A K Q J 10 8 7
                ◇ 10
                ♣ Q
```

The bidding:

West	North	East	South
Helgemo	*Lund*	*Tislevoll*	*Osbak*
—	1♣	Pass	1♡
1♠	2♣	Pass	4♡
All Pass			

The bidding was unremarkable and was duplicated at most of the tables. And the contract of Four Hearts was made everywhere since West led the ace of diamonds and East no longer had the chance to get two spade ruffs, as West had already used up his diamond entry. Everybody took the blow philosophically and expected no swing, since it was surely impossible to find any lead but the top diamond. But not for Geir Helgemo.

To explain what really happened I must tell you something about our carding methods. Our defence is based upon encouraging and discouraging signals, and not so much on giving count. Many players give count more frequently than is standard amongst the top players in Trondheim. Of course, it is arguable as to what is best in the long run, and players from the upper elite in the rest of the world do things a little differently from us.

In Trondheim we stick to our principles. For instance, we encourage from a doubleton on partner's lead of the ace (ace from ace-king) when we wish partner to play ace, king and another for us to ruff. We do that even if the dummy shows up with Q-x-x or more. For us to signal something other than encouraging/discouraging there needs to be a clear-cut shift situation, and if so, we use a Lavinthal signal. These are Helgemo's preferred methods as well, although I know that from time to time he plays differently when partnering foreigners.

By the way, we play low cards as encouraging. Again, it probably does not matter so much how you play these things, as long as you have agreed them properly with your partner.

On the actual hand shown above, to beat Four Hearts West needed to find the lead of the ace of spades from A-J-x-x-x when holding A-K-Q of another suit. Who would make such a spectacular lead? Answer: Geir Helgemo. He had figured out this lie of the cards, and, believe it or not, the ace of spades was on the table in front of him only a few seconds after the bidding was over. For sure, in 999 out of 1,000 cases he would have switched to a diamond honour at trick two but, as he said, it did not matter which quick trick he took first. This time he was extremely lucky because he saw the two of spades from his partner, encouraging. The probability that this was a singleton was very good, since with a doubleton (seeing the king in dummy) or three-card spade suit partner should have discouraged. So it was clearly the right moment to crown an unbelievable defence when Geir continued with his jack of spades at trick two. Impressed?

This was one of the darker regions of our trip to Helgemo's world of bridge. The defence I have just written about was designed to impress … but it was also impressively stupid. For yet again I have switched some cards between the East and South hands. This was the true hand:

Petter Osbak

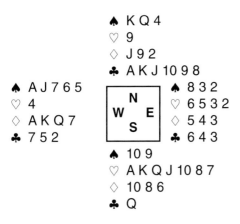

I was sitting East with just about as bad a hand as possible. I was doing little else but wait for the next board. Seconds later it was very plain that I had made a great fool of myself. My thought – if it can be called that – was that since I had no wish for my partner to shift to another suit I should simply play the two, encouraging. As soon as I had done that a huge present was given to declarer, since when Geir continued spades it let declarer win the second trick, and now he could take twelve tricks in his no-play game!

I should, of course, have discouraged in spades. I could see dummy's clubs and, even though I did not hold anything in

diamonds, I should not have encouraged. The maestro asked whether I liked spades or not, and I should have told him. Not such a tough question to answer!

It can certainly be dangerous to play with Helgemo, and it does not matter whether you have a good or a bad hand.

After this fiasco there were a few dull hands, and then, as if our opponents felt sorry for me, they bid a slam missing two aces. We managed to cash our tricks and the match score was levelled. On the last hand of the session I was again dealt a lousy hand:

♠ 2
♡ 9 8 7 6
♢ J 9 6 2
♣ J 8 6 5

Everybody was vulnerable and Geir opened Two Clubs, strong artificial. I remember thinking: here we go again…

North, Børre Lund, bid Two Spades and it was my turn. I began feeling worried. Fresh in my mind was the worthless hand I had held when defending the Four Heart contract a few boards ago. But I was quite sure I remembered our agreement after the opponents intervened over our strong Two Clubs. Double was the weakest action (showing 0–3 HCP). So I doubled, and Osbak bid Four Spades. Geir passed, showing some extras, since with a minimum he would surely have doubled Four Spades. That meant he was interested in playing a contract our way instead of defending. Lund also passed and it was my turn in fourth seat. I had to bid something and double was surely wrong with a singleton spade, so I chose Four No-Trumps – which I hoped partner would read as a hand with at least two places to play. But Geir seemed to be happy to play somewhere I had not considered, because after a pass from Osbak, Geir also passed!

My heart seemed to stop for a few beats, but fortunately it soon started up again. I tried to calm down. He probably knew what he was doing, but rather surprisingly it looked as if I might be declarer in Four No-Trumps with this powerhouse!

Børre Lund

However, the bidding was not yet over. Lund bid Five Spades and again it was my turn. What now? If I passed partner would maybe believe I had a maximum for what I had shown so far, and I certainly could have held a king or some combination of minor honours, or even, for instance, a 5-5 distribution. A pass should be stronger than double in this situation, even though partner had passed Four No-Trumps. Let's say a void in spades, or a 5-5 hand … so I doubled, trying to warn my man.

The atmosphere was electric, and I could feel pearls of sweat sliding down my brows. I was holding a hand only 2 points, but so far I had doubled twice and bid Four No-Trumps! After pass from the next hand Geir paused. Please pass, I was thinking. Please pass! But he paused for some more seconds, and suddenly the bell saved us.

Loud and clear for us all to hear, a player at the next table said, 'I should have gone on to Six Diamonds, partner. Sorry.' It had to be this hand, since none of the previous boards had included a problem of this type. Geir held a solid seven-card diamond suit and was trying to guess between pass, Five No-Trumps and Six Diamonds. But the hand was ruined for us. We now knew the right thing to do was to continue to Six Diamonds because of the stentorian player next to us. So the director was called and he correctly cancelled the board in our match. What would have happened we will never know, but Five Spades was cold and both Five No-Trumps and Six Diamonds were good sacrifices for us.

I was happy the match was over. It ended with a small victory for us (17–13 VP). With more such boring hands what else could we expect?

Although many hands in this chapter have shown Geir Helgemo collect bad scores, his creativity is still fascinating. And he needs it in many situations, not only at the bridge table.

An example of that is an incident that happened after the World Junior Pairs Championship in Ghent, Belgium. Geir and Boye Brogeland won, their first World Championship title, and a historic triumph for Norwegian bridge. This just had to be celebrated in a proper way.

After a big party, Geir had to leave early the next morning without a wink of sleep. Another bridge tournament was awaiting him somewhere. At six o'clock in the morning he left by train, and his first stop was the airport in Brussels. Since he had not had a second's sleep you can imagine he was very tired, so he took a nap, but when he woke up the newly crowned world champion was not at the airport in Brussels. His train was far away, somewhere inside the Netherlands! He had no money, just his airline ticket and a suitcase full of dirty clothes. And he was heading away from his destination. What was he to do? Good advice was now at a premium. But a world champion does not give in that easily. He jumped off the train at the next station, and boarded a train going in the opposite direction. He had no ticket, but the idea of going to sleep again was a good one. This time it was not a genuine nap, but it was good enough to fool the conductors. Every time they passed, Geir's eyes were closed, and his cheek on his chest. It worked. The tired champion caught his plane and was soon heading for his next bridge adventure.

The illusionist

Some years ago a training tournament was played in Trondheim to prepare the Norwegian team before an international event. In the actual competition a few weeks later they did very well, but in the training session things did not go so well. The reason was probably that they were lacking motivation. It's not the same playing against friends in the Bridgehouse in Trondheim, with no screens, few spectators, and no prizes or titles to play for. I played on the team of 'local stars' who formed the opposition. We certainly felt it was exciting to play the best team in the country and there were no motivation problems for our squad. My partner was Gunnar Voie, a player who can, on his good days, 'kill' anyone. But on this hand you will probably agree he had no chance of finding the solution.

Gunnar Voie

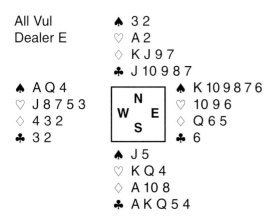

All Vul	♠ 3 2
Dealer E	♡ A 2
	◇ K J 9 7
	♣ J 10 9 8 7

The bidding:

West	North	East	South
Helgemo	*Tislevoll*	*Helness*	*Voie*
—	—	2♠	Dble
3♠	Dble	Pass	5♣
All Pass			

Helness opened a weak Two, and the double was for take-out. The double of

Three Spades showed both minors and Voie bid what he thought he could make. Five Clubs was an excellent contract, just depending on the view in diamonds.

Now we come to the creation of illusions. Geir Helgemo made the spectacular lead of the queen of spades. A lead of the queen from ace-queen-small is obviously far from standard against a game contract at the five level. So why did he do that?

Look how impossible it makes life for declarer. The queen of spades scored the first trick and next came a spade to the king. East switched to trumps. I would have liked to partner a declarer who in this position could rationally have guessed the diamond position. From declarer's point of view East held the ace-king of spades. In which case, how do you play diamonds? In abstract it would often be right to finesse in a side suit against the partner of the weak Two opener. And when the weak hand has already shown an ace and a king, the choice of plays in the side suit is obvious. It is next to impossible for declarer to expose this deceptive defensive play. And that is very often the case in Helgemo's world of bridge. But things did not exactly work out according to plan.

A few cards were switched in my first diagram to illustrate the point. This was the full hand in the real world:

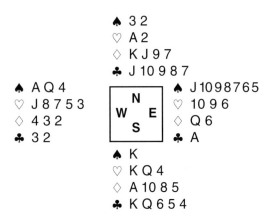

```
              ♠ 3 2
              ♡ A 2
              ◇ K J 9 7
              ♣ J 10 9 8 7
♠ A Q 4                      ♠ J 10 9 8 7 6 5
♡ J 8 7 5 3        N         ♡ 10 9 6
◇ 4 3 2        W     E       ◇ Q 6
♣ 3 2             S          ♣ A
              ♠ K
              ♡ K Q 4
              ◇ A 10 8 5
              ♣ K Q 6 5 4
```

You never know, perhaps Voie would have guessed the diamonds and made his game contract if Geir had cashed the ace of spades at trick one. But if at trick two Geir had continued with the four of spades to Tor's jack, maybe declarer would have misguessed diamonds for the same reason as in the false picture Geir tried to create. Before declarer commits himself he can find out that East holds the ace of clubs as well, and the first two tricks may suggest that East holds a better

spade combination than he actually does. Surely no one could blame declarer for playing West for the queen of diamonds?

However, one way to play the hand would be by cashing three rounds of hearts before exiting in trumps. Such a play would be wrong if hearts were 6-2, but as the cards lay here this would have been the winning move. East would have been endplayed with his singleton ace of clubs and would have to help declarer find the queen of diamonds.

Mind you, with Helgemo in the West seat, after his ace of spades had dropped declarer's king he would surely have switched to a club immediately to stop the endplay.

The lead of the queen of spades was itself a stroke of genius. Geir understood that if the Five Club contract was to be beaten, declarer would have to be fooled. Normally there would be no danger in leading the queen of partner's suit, because the weak Two opener usually has one of the three top honours. Their agreements were normally not to open pre-empts with a weak suit, but this time Tor chose to do so because of the seventh spade and the defensive values outside. And that is why this creative lead became the subject of derisive laughter rather than applause, and the kibitzers got the opportunity to shake their heads and claim that they would never have made such a mistake.

More system discussion

I am sure you now understand that discussions about system are not Geir Helgemo's favourite pursuit, but just before the 1996 European Pairs Championship Geir and I prepared quite hard. We had not played much together and we actually spent some hours agreeing a reasonable system.

One of the conventions we agreed to use was what we called 'minor-suit Stayman' over partner's One No-Trump opening. But we got no further than mentioning the name of the convention during our discussion. However, it came up in the very first session of the championship. With South as dealer, both vulnerable, I held as North:

♠ 5 4
♡ 2
◇ K 10 9 8 7 5
♣ 7 4 3 2

Geir opened One No-Trump (15–17 HCP) and West passed. We used red-suit transfers so Two Spades was available as the minor-suit enquiry. The standard way of using that convention in Trondheim was that responder could hold either one or both minors when using the convention, with a weak or strong hand. Over the Two Spade bid the no-trump opener is supposed to bid Two No-Trumps with better (longer) diamonds or approximately equal minor suits. Over Two No-Trumps, responder shows a weak hand with a long suit by bidding Three Clubs or Three Diamonds. Responder can make a higher bid with some kind of stronger minor hand. This was the way I had played 'minor-suit Stayman' since before Geir Helgemo could walk.

Here I bid Two Spades, intending to play in Three Diamonds whatever

response I got. But when the bidding tray came back under the screen I got a small shock. The Three Diamond bid was in front of Geir. According to the system he was not allowed to make that bid, for I might have had a long club suit and nothing else. This time, though, there was no problem since I held diamonds, and so passing did not require much thought. Geir made ten tricks, and surprisingly it proved to be close to a top.

He had valued his 14 HCP hand with a good five-card diamond suit as 15, and we had stolen the hand! Our opponents could make eleven tricks in hearts, and with a normal One Diamond opening bid they would easily have reached that spot. Our best result would then have been to sacrifice for at least minus 200. The bidding, using our undefined minor-suit Stayman convention, could have ended in disaster for us on a different day. Instead we got one of our best scores of the session.

Without wanting to start a discussion on the matter, I had to ask Geir before the next round why he had bid Three Diamonds. Geir looked confused. For him Stayman meant asking for a four-card suit, so why shouldn't he tell me about his five-card suit? Stayman means Stayman, was the answer. End of discussion.

The way Geir wanted to use the minor-suit enquiry could certainly work. When responder has slam ambitions it can be especially valuable to know that opener has at least a four-card suit in one of the minors. I understood we now had an agreement, and did not worry any more about it, hoping a weak hand with long clubs would not show up opposite a no-trump opening. But more than a year later we got into minor-suit Stayman trouble again.

Every autumn the bridge season starts in mid-Norway with a popular tournament called the Namsos Cup. Geir and I played in it several times, and a strange episode happened in 1997. Halfway through the first day an elderly couple entered the playing rooms. When they saw that Geir Helgemo was playing, the man pointed directly at Geir and dragged his wife towards our table. Soon they were sitting behind their idol to watch what they expected to be top-class bridge. Only a few minutes later they had the chance to see a ridiculous board, so unbelievable that they might have imagined that the players involved were beginners. The couple were shocked.

This was what happened, as seen from my point of view. I was dealer with both sides vulnerable:

♠ K 10 3 2
♡ A 10
♢ A 10 9 8 7
♣ K 10

Buoyed by my intermediates, I opened a slightly unorthodox One No-Trump bid, showing a little more in high-card points than I held. Geir responded Two Clubs, Stayman, and the next hand overcalled Two Hearts. I showed my spades and Geir said Three Clubs, another enquiry about my distribution. Three Diamonds was my response, showing a second four-card suit. Geir's next bid was Three Spades, natural and a slam invitation. Since I held 14 HCP and had promised 15–17 I signed off in Four Spades.

Seconds after bidding only game I realised my bad judgement. In a spade contract the hand should be evaluated quite highly rather than as a dead minimum. A cue-bid is, in fact, obvious over Three Spades and I now started worrying that we might miss a good

slam. But after a short hesitation Geir came back with Four No-Trumps, Roman Key Card Blackwood. I can remember thinking at the time: there is no danger of missing a slam by making a slight underbid with this guy. He'll take up the slack for you anyway.

Spades were trumps so I bid Five Clubs, three aces out of five (including the trump king). Then came a big surprise: everybody passed! Geir's fan club had eyes blinking like traffic lights. They did not believe what they saw. Something had gone completely crazy. I could hardly restrain myself from laughing at their reaction. Instead of laughing, I asked for permission to go to the men's room and started laughing in there. When I came back to the table the hand was over. Geir had gone three down, minus 300. 'I misplayed the trumps,' he said, sounding as if he had just played in the standard contract. I simply had to see his cards, and they were:

♠ 9 4
♡ 5 3
♢ J 6
♣ Q 9 8 7 6 5 2

A totally ridiculous bidding sequence, but the result was not too bad for us. East/West could make game in hearts; actually quite a few pairs had done so. But what had happened at our table? Had the bridge genius gone crazy? Our kibitzers never received an explanation that day, but if they read this book they will maybe understand. The bidding is repeated so you can follow the explanation more easily:

West	North	East	South
—	1NT	Pass	2♣ (!)
2♡	2♠	Pass	3♣ (!!)
Pass	3♢	Pass	3♠ (!!!)
Pass	4♠	Pass	4NT (!!!!)
Pass	5♣	All Pass	

When looking only at the bidding, everything looks normal up to the pass of Five Clubs. Spades are established as trumps, so the pass just looks like a misbid. What did Helgemo intend by his cryptic bidding?

The problem stemmed from our 'minor-suit Stayman' difficulties mentioned earlier. The way Geir wanted to use the minor-suit enquiry, left him with no way of playing in a club partscore, because over the Two Spade asking bid he risked getting the response of Three Diamonds. Instead he chose a creative but quite dangerous way of trying to settle in a club contract. His idea was to hope for a response of Two Hearts over Two Clubs. In that case he could bid Two No-Trumps, an artificial asking bid. Over that Two No-Trump asking bid the responses are a bit strange, since Three Clubs shows diamonds, Three Diamonds five hearts, and Three Hearts four spades. We do this to get more space for making slam tries. He was hoping for something like the following sequence:

1NT	2♣
2♡	2NT

The probability of getting a Three Club response over Two No-Trumps was quite good, since it showed diamonds, the Man thought, given the cards he held himself. He would in that case happily pass it out.

I agree that it was silly not to have a better system to cover the actual hand he held, but this was a smart solution, was it not? I guess you are shaking your head now. Of course, genius is close to insanity – and maybe Geir crossed the line here. And things became even messier when I bid Two Spades instead of the Two Hearts he was hoping for. But he did not give up. Three Clubs was a new relay, and Three

Spades a natural slam try. At this point the kibitzing couple probably started to believe Mr Helgemo was drunk, but he bid as he did quite deliberately. His intention was to pass out a probable response of Four Clubs, the cue-bid I should have made! But no, I woodenly raised to Four Spades.

Helgemo still refused to give up. His last chance was to try Roman Key Card Blackwood. At last he ran into some good luck, since the response was Five Clubs, showing three aces. Finally, partner bid clubs, but it took five rounds of bidding. It was not surprising that the old couple now had eyes as big as tin plates.

I travelled home from this tournament with Terje Aa and Glenn Grøtheim. When I told them about this bidding horror story Terje could not breathe because he was laughing so hard, and Glenn had problems keeping the car on the road. The rest of the way home we thought it safer to talk about something other than bridge.

Some months after the horror story in the Namsos Cup we were going to Bergen to play in the Premier League. On the plane one of our classic system discussions occurred. As we found our seats Geir said:

'Geo, I think there is one systemic change we can agree to.'

'Oh yes?' I answered, a bit perplexed. Was Geir beginning to take system discussions seriously?

I put away the newspaper I had just opened, and looked at him, interested in what he was going to say. He said:

'From now on we will use the minor ask of Two Spades the way you suggested some while ago.'

That was all. Then he took *my* newspaper, opened it, and started reading. Happily, soon after the stewardess came with refreshments.

A personal worst

The next hand may represent Geir's worst ever penalty at the bridge table. It contains a Blackwood sequence that no one else understood. Or was it Blackwood at all?

But first of all I must mention another Blackwood blunder. In a junior championship Geir and the brilliant Ole Berset arrived in a situation where the response to Blackwood could have shown zero or three aces, and the other guy could not tell which, although no aces were unlikely from the bidding thus far. The standard way to solve such an unusual problem is to sign off and then the other player will bid on if he has three aces. The impatient juniors had no time for such science; it takes a few seconds to make a bid at the five level, does it not – good drinking time wasted! Do you think the grand slam made? Not at all. The grand slam would have been laydown if the responder to Blackwood had held three aces, but unfortunately he did not. Head-shaking opponents cashed out for three down, doubled, and Geir and his partner sat there looking forlornly at their kings, queens and jacks.

But Geir's worst tragedy came on home ground, in the Bridgehouse in Trondheim. This was the deal:

NS Vul
Dealer S

	♠ 4	
	♡ 5 2	
	◇ Q 10 5 3	
	♣ J 9 8 6 4 3	

♠ K 10 9 8 7 5 3 2		♠ J 6
♡ K 6	N	♡ 9 8 7
◇ —	W E	◇ K J 9 8 6 2
♣ 7 5 2	S	♣ A K

	♠ A Q	
	♡ A Q J 10 4 3	
	◇ A 7 4	
	♣ Q 10	

This was the bidding – and yes, everyone was sober:

West	North	East	South
			Geir
—	—	—	2♣
4♠	Pass	Pass	4NT
Pass	5♣	5♠	Pass
Pass	6♣	Dble	6NT
Pass	Pass	Dble	All Pass

I'll spare you the explanations. The result speaks for itself. The defence was spectacular; a club lead and a spade switch! Helgemo went nine down, doubled, for a score of minus 2600. Something about whether the pass of Five Spades was forcing or invitational was mentioned, but I think it is kinder to let it pass in silence. Maybe North's pass over Four Spades was read as stronger than if he had doubled. Many players like using the double as the weakest response when partner opens Two Clubs and the opponents overcall. However, in this case something went completely wrong. I was in the same room when this happened, and remember very well that Ekren and Helgemo were the ones who laughed the loudest.

If you think parts of this chapter are a little unkind to Mr Helgemo, I can only say that I wanted to provide balance and show in a humorous way that no-one is perfect.

Part Five

The Defender

Helgemo with Pil Austberg

Killing lead

Although Helgemo is expert in all areas of the game, where he impresses most is in his defence. If you, his partner, manage to keep up, it will result in bridge at its most rewarding. It is sometimes difficult early in the game to guess what he is up to. He is always ahead of the rest, often starting to create traps for his opponents before they have seen a problem at all. Sometimes it looks as if he has played the board before. Indeed, it is often difficult for others to see the killing defence even when looking at all four hands. The key to this is a fabulous deductive ability. Geir always creates a picture of the full hand in his mind. Sometimes it seems as if, before the lead is made, he knows exactly where to attack and what kind of problems declarer will have later on.

A good lead is a good start to a defence. Many players seem to think it is a coincidence whether or not a lead works well, but Geir seldom makes the wrong lead. And when he chooses a spectacular lead he often hit's the bull's eye.

Many people follow Helgemo's bridge by reading bulletins, bridge magazines and newspaper columns, which often focus on the extraordinary. That is why it is understandable when people believe that Geir frequently underleads aces against suit contracts, for example. It is not true. I know many players who try that sort of thing much more often. The point is that when Geir does it the lead works! The newspapers then tell of those stories and that kind of lead appears to happen much more frequently than it really does.

The first hand in this chapter was played in a local tournament. It happened shortly after Geir returned from playing the Spring Nationals in the USA. The Shugart team had reached the semi-finals, but lost. In spite of that disappointment Geir agreed to play in a couple of minor spring tournaments in Norway. Per Erik Austberg, a young talent who later played internationally for Norway, was Geir's partner. Helgemo and Austberg won those local events in spite of a hard professional session the previous week. No problems with motivation for Helgemo!

I kibitzed Austberg and Helgemo for a couple of hours, and I got what I wanted.

```
None Vul        ♠ A 9 6
Dealer S        ♡ K 8 6 2
                ◊ 8 4
                ♣ A 6 5 2
              ┌─────────┐
              │    N    │
              │ W     E │
              │    S    │
              └─────────┘
                ♠ K Q 8
                ♡ Q J 3
                ◊ A K 10
                ♣ K Q 10 7
```

South opened Two No-Trumps (20–21 HCP) and fnished up in Six No-Trumps. Six Clubs would have been a better contract, but at matchpoints the no-trump slam seemed a fair shot from North's point of view. The contract needed three heart tricks and a reasonable lie in clubs. In addition, there were some possibilities in diamonds, although it looks difficult to combine all the different chances. South was a young and inexperienced player, but he understood that the heart suit was critical.

The ten of hearts was led from West and the lead made South quite optimistic. He took the first trick with the queen when East followed low. Then declarer continued with his jack of hearts, which went to East's ace when West followed with the five. The diamond switch was taken in hand and a heart played towards dummy. West followed with the seven of hearts. South asked confidently for the eight of hearts from dummy, but he got a shock when East produced the nine, which was supposed to be with West! This was the full deal:

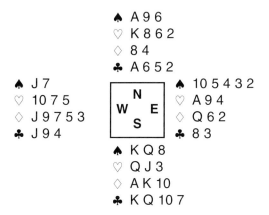

```
              ♠ A 9 6
              ♡ K 8 6 2
              ◇ 8 4
              ♣ A 6 5 2
♠ J 7                        ♠ 10 5 4 3 2
♡ 10 7 5        N            ♡ A 9 4
◇ J 9 7 5 3  W   E           ◇ Q 6 2
♣ J 9 4        S             ♣ 8 3
              ♠ K Q 8
              ♡ Q J 3
              ◇ A K 10
              ♣ K Q 10 7
```

South was unlucky but not clever enough. His problem was that he didn't consider it was possible that the lead could be from 10-x-x. It needs good imagination for the player with 10-7-5 to think of it, but even more for declarer. If he had considered the possibility he would, of course, have entered dummy and played a low heart towards his hand, a much better shot than playing the jack of hearts from hand. If the hearts were as he believed, 10-9-x-x with West, the ace would have shown up when he played a small heart from dummy. As it was, East, with A-9, would have had no chance of making life difficult for declarer since the nine or ace would have to be played.

Who was West? You have probably guessed. In one of the breaks I asked

Geir why he thought of leading the ten from such a combination. His answer was, as always, simple, but a question itself:

'Can you tell me what is a tempting lead from my hand?'

He was right. Nothing was tempting. Everything seems to be well placed and a row of jacks will fall. Leading the ten from such a holding is unusual, but can cause a problem for declarer who may believe the opening leader holds the nine. Every time East holds the nine and an honour the lead sets up a dangerous position.

To underlead an ace against a suit contract can be a double-edged sword. Some players try it often. Sometimes it works and they are so pleased with themselves that they forget all the times it doesn't. When Helgemo does try such a lead it usually works.

This was what South was exposed to in the final of the 1992 Norwegian Teams Championship.

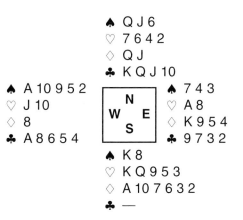

```
              ♠ Q J 6
              ♡ 7 6 4 2
              ◇ Q J
              ♣ K Q J 10
♠ A 10 9 5 2                 ♠ 7 4 3
♡ J 10         N            ♡ A 8
◇ 8         W   E            ◇ K 9 5 4
♣ A 8 6 5 4    S             ♣ 9 7 3 2
              ♠ K 8
              ♡ K Q 9 5 3
              ◇ A 10 7 6 3 2
              ♣ —
```

South ended up in Four Hearts after choosing to open One Heart. Over Geir's One Spade overcall North invited the heart game. South made a mild slam try before stopping in game.

The bidding suggested to Geir that something special was needed to beat the

Repeated
for
convenience

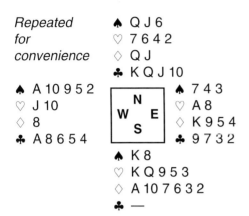

♠ Q J 6
♡ 7 6 4 2
◇ Q J
♣ K Q J 10

♠ A 10 9 5 2   ♠ 7 4 3
♡ J 10   ♡ A 8
◇ 8   ◇ K 9 5 4
♣ A 8 6 5 4   ♣ 9 7 3 2

♠ K 8
♡ K Q 9 5 3
◇ A 10 7 6 3 2
♣ —

Terje Aa

contract. That's why he rejected the standard lead of the singleton diamond, the lead that was made at all the other tables. Later Geir told me that if he had known his partner held the ace of hearts he probably would have led his singleton. But on the diamond lead the game contract was made at every table. East got in with his trump ace and gave his partner a ruff, but the ace of spades was all there was to come. But not where Geir was West.

As if Geir knew all this in advance he instead tried the lead of the four of clubs. Declarer won the trick with his king, and, with no useful discard, he let go a diamond. If you or I had tried that lead, declarer would probably have had a singleton club.

In Helgemo's world it was different. At trick two South played a heart to the king and the ten fell from West. From South's point of view it was probable that the trumps were 3-1, and he wanted to play another trump from dummy. South continued with the king of spades, which was allowed to hold the trick. Geir took the next spade and then placed the ace of clubs on the table! Declarer ruffed, and the way the defence had gone convinced him the trumps were 3-1. Or else, why was West so eager to refuse him an entry to dummy? However, South believed he knew the right counter move. Dummy's

diamond combination was a probable entry, so he decided to play a small diamond to the queen.

It was not a good idea. East won a trick he should never have made with his king of diamonds and continued the suit for West to ruff. The trump ace could not disappear and that was the fourth defensive trick. Declarer went one down in a contract that appeared to be laydown, and you really have to feel sorry for him.

The following year Helgemo played in his first open world championship. Norway did very well in the Bermuda Bowl in Santiago. Geir partnered Tor Helness, and the team also contained another pair from Trondheim, Terje Aa and Glenn Grøtheim. The third pair was Jon Sveindal and Arild Rasmussen from Bergen. Many people were surprised when the Norwegians kept on winning all the way to the final. Then they met the Netherlands, a team we had shown on several occasions that we could beat. Gold medals were certainly possible. But it was not to be. In the final our young team looked tired and had to settle for silver. Still, it was an excellent effort.

The very first card Geir Helgemo put on the table in this championship was lethal. Young Helgemo, aged 23, was already a star back home in Norway. In the rest of Europe people had also begun to discover him, but in the States he was unknown. To them he was probably considered just another promising junior. So Peter Weichsel and Bobby Levin got quite a surprise on this deal.

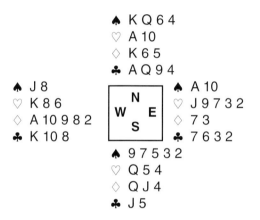

```
                 ♠ K Q 6 4
                 ♡ A 10
                 ◇ K 6 5
                 ♣ A Q 9 4
  ♠ J 8                      ♠ A 10
  ♡ K 8 6          N         ♡ J 9 7 3 2
  ◇ A 10 9 8 2  W     E      ◇ 7 3
  ♣ K 10 8          S         ♣ 7 6 3 2
                 ♠ 9 7 5 3 2
                 ♡ Q 5 4
                 ◇ Q J 4
                 ♣ J 5
```

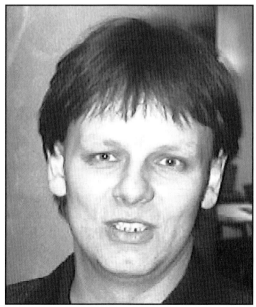

Arild Rasmussen

In the standard auction to Four Spades, North had revealed a balanced hand with 18–19 HCP and four spades. As if he had seen the cards beforehand, Geir led the ten of diamonds. Declarer won the trick and played on trumps. But when Helness was in with the ace of trumps, he played a diamond to the ace and got his ruff. Helness exited with a club, leaving hearts well alone, so declarer later had to concede a heart trick; one down and a dynamic start for Norway.

Spectacular leads are fascinating when they succeed. Sometimes, however, although they give declarer an extra trick, he may be perplexed because of it, and give back what he was given and more besides. This is an amusing hand from the 1995 European Pairs Championship.

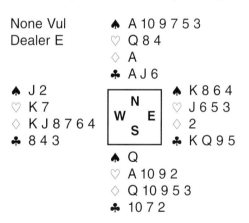

```
None Vul         ♠ A 10 9 7 5 3
Dealer E         ♡ Q 8 4
                 ◇ A
                 ♣ A J 6
  ♠ J 2                      ♠ K 8 6 4
  ♡ K 7            N         ♡ J 6 5 3
  ◇ K J 8 7 6 4  W     E     ◇ 2
  ♣ 8 4 3          S         ♣ K Q 9 5
                 ♠ Q
                 ♡ A 10 9 2
                 ◇ Q 10 9 5 3
                 ♣ 10 7 2
```

Sitting East I opened a Norwegian Two Diamonds (we had not yet abandoned it), showing both majors and a weak hand (below opening strength). After two passes North bid Two Spades, natural, South tried Two No-Trumps and North raised to game. Our opponents had reached a thin game, but with all hands on view it is hard to see how we could beat the contract.

Geir had a difficult lead against Three No-Trumps. Many would probably have tried a diamond, hoping partner could produce the queen. But it's not exactly tempting, even though this time it may well have been best since North held the singleton ace. A club lead would also have worked well this time. However, declarer can make a lot of tricks whatever the lead, due to the fortunate spade situation. The lead was a guess, and Geir guessed something special. He wanted to put me in to play diamonds through declarer and his choice was the seven of hearts, low from honour doubleton against a no-trump contract! In his head he was hoping I could produce the ace and switch to a diamond – what a daring defence. But the layout was not exactly what he had hoped for …

South played small from dummy and I put in the jack. Declarer now had three secure heart tricks but, because of the bidding and lead, he was convinced I had both the heart honours. To keep communications between the hands he let me hold the trick with the jack.

No luck! Next came the three of hearts from me and declarer let it ride, his intention being to take the trick with his queen. But Geir shocked declarer by producing the king. South could have recovered later on, but after this start he was psyched out. And, you must admit, he would have felt very bad giving away two heart tricks from this combination after getting a heart lead! When the smoke had cleared, a shocked South had gone two down.

By 1997 Geir had found his place at the top of international bridge. However, the opponents' recognition of his abilities adds an extra element to the confrontation. In the Bermuda Bowl in Tunisia the great Italian player Lorenzo Lauria certainly knew Helgemo's reputation:

Lorenzo Lauria

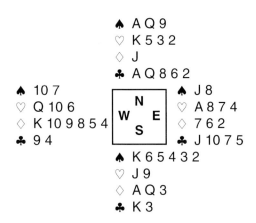

Lauria was declarer in the good contract of Six Spades. His opponents had been silent. Geir was on lead and he put the ten of hearts on the table.

Lauria was faced with an awkward choice. He knew Geir was quite capable of leading the ten from A-10 or Q-10 and it probably felt like a fifty-fifty guess. If East held both the heart honours there was, of course, no hope. After a long pause the Italian put up the king and was one down in a slam that would otherwise have been laydown.

Working together

One important fact in successful defence is … your partner. The player sitting opposite you has to understand what's going on. Many brilliant defences vanish because of one partner 'sleeping'. However, when Helgemo is on top form he is very good at making things easy for his partner. This is an important ability. It is not enough to execute a few brilliant coups, if the partnership's everyday defence is not functioning well. Long tournaments mostly consist of everyday hands.

Of course, Helgemo has mostly partnered good players. Tony Forrester and Tor Helness have already been mentioned, and they are world-class players. Some of the defences Helgemo has produced with those two could reasonably be described as works of art. However, I will start with a hand where Helness made one of his few blunders.

Jan Westerhof

♠ Q 5 4 3
♡ Q 3 2
♢ A 4
♣ Q 10 9 8

```
      N
  W       E
      S
```

♠ K J 6
♡ A K 7 4
♢ Q J 6
♣ K 5 4

The hand occurred in the World Teams Olympiad in Rhodes. South was the strong Dutch player Jan Westerhof. He was declaring the standard contract of Three No-Trumps. A low diamond was led from Helgemo (West). Try putting yourself in the Dutchman's seat.

Westerhof put up the ace of diamonds and played a spade to the king which held. Then he played a club to the queen. East produced the ace and returned the ten of spades. South covered with the jack and West took the ace before continuing with the nine to dummy's queen. On the third round of spades East discarded a heart so declarer knew West held the master seven of spades. Westerhof played a diamond to the queen which held, West following with the five, East having played a discouraging nine followed by the seven. Declarer had eight top tricks and could get his ninth either from a simple club finesse, or by finding the hearts 3-3. But on the second round of hearts West showed out, discarding the eight of diamonds. Then, on the third round of hearts the ten of diamonds. How do you think the cards are lying?

Westerhof had no doubt. West probably held an originally 4-1-5-3 distribution, and was now down to the bare king of diamonds. The reason he had kept his two remaining clubs was, of course, that he had started with J-x-x. It was time to endplay Helgemo; after he had made his spade and diamond tricks he would have to lead a club. However, the whole thing was just an illusion for the Dutchman. This was the full deal:

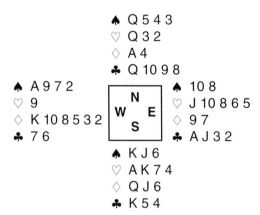

♠ Q 5 4 3
♡ Q 3 2
◇ A 4
♣ Q 10 9 8

♠ A 9 7 2   ♠ 10 8
♡ 9   ♡ J 10 8 6 5
◇ K 10 8 5 3 2   ◇ 9 7
♣ 7 6   ♣ A J 3 2

♠ K J 6
♡ A K 7 4
◇ Q J 6
♣ K 5 4

When East was in with the ace of clubs he should have cleared the diamonds and the contract would have been doomed. The spade continuation meant declarer had a chance to succeed. As Geir's entry for the diamonds had been knocked out he had to go for an alternative plan.

He set up his spade trick and then later let the queen of diamonds hold. Note that if he had taken that trick and cashed the seven of spades declarer cannot go wrong. If he throws a heart and later takes the club finesse it will work, and if he instead throws the five of clubs West will exit in a red suit. When declarer makes his diamond trick East must give up his club or heart stopper. That is why Geir ducked. It allowed declarer to go for the endplay but when he was thrown in Geir cashed both a spade trick *and* the deuce of diamonds and the defenders had five tricks for one down.

I do not wish to give the wrong impression about Helness, who is normally a good and accurate defender. Watch this hand from the Cap Gemini Tournament.

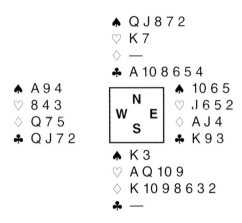

♠ Q J 8 7 2
♡ K 7
◇ —
♣ A 10 8 6 5 4

♠ A 9 4   ♠ 10 6 5
♡ 8 4 3   ♡ J 6 5 2
◇ Q 7 5   ◇ A J 4
♣ Q J 7 2   ♣ K 9 3

♠ K 3
♡ A Q 10 9
◇ K 10 9 8 6 3 2
♣ —

South played in Three No-Trumps, having shown his diamond suit and a minimum opening hand. Helness (West) found the best lead, the two of clubs. Declarer played low from dummy and Helgemo won the trick with his nine. East switched to a heart. South won with the ten, and played on spades. Helness won the third round and played another heart to dummy's singleton king. Declarer was helpless. This was the ending after the spades were cashed:

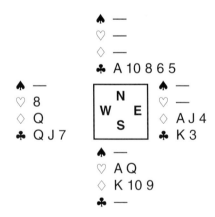

♠ —
♡ —
◇ —
♣ A 10 8 6 5

♠ —   ♠ —
♡ 8   ♡ —
◇ Q   ◇ A J 4
♣ Q J 7   ♣ K 3

♠ —
♡ A Q
◇ K 10 9
♣ —

Declarer cashed the ace of clubs, but Geir was quick to throw his king under it. South let a diamond go. The next club was won by West and South threw the queen of hearts. But on the last club from West, South was squeezed. With only two cards left he could choose between blanking his king of diamonds and seeing East taking the rest in that suit, or throwing his last heart and letting West take a trick with his eight. The defensive squeeze beat the contract by two.

One of Helgemo's specialities is to create the illusion that the hand is completely different from what it really is. In 1990 Norway won the Junior European Championship and this hand is from their match against Israel which effectively decided the final outcome.

Ole Berset

♠ K 10
♡ J 3 2
◇ A Q J 8 6 2
♣ J 8

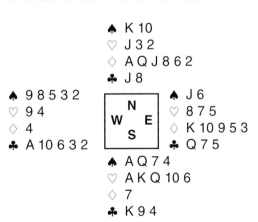

♠ A Q 7 4
♡ A K Q 10 6
◇ 7
♣ K 9 4

South became declarer in Six Hearts having shown a strong hand by reversing, showing four spades and five hearts. North had bid a Two-over-One in diamonds before supporting hearts.

West was the super talent Ole Berset from Sunndalsøra and East Geir Helgemo. On this deal Ole did not find the best lead when he chose the ace of clubs. The next club went to the jack, queen and king, and declarer ruffed his small club. Then he made an error: he played a small trump to his ten before going after the spade suit. A spade to the king and a spade back to the ace was followed by ruffing a spade with the trump jack. Because of that unnecessary earlier round of trumps, declarer was now out of trumps in dummy, and needed to get back to his hand to draw trumps. The ace of diamonds was cashed and the ten dropped from East. Then on the next

small diamond from dummy Geir produced the king! South was at the crossroads. If he ruffed high he was dependent on a 3-2 trump break. And if the king of diamonds was really a doubleton East was 2-2 in spades and diamonds, something that made it less likely that trumps were 3-2. South ruffed with his six of hearts and a happy Berset overruffed, then a spade ruff by East took the contract two down. This was the full deal:

♠ K 10
♡ J 3 2
◇ A Q J 8 6 2
♣ J 8

♠ 9 8 5 3 2   ♠ J 6
♡ 9 4   ♡ 8 7 5
◇ 4   ◇ K 10 9 5 3
♣ A 10 6 3 2   ♣ Q 7 5

♠ A Q 7 4
♡ A K Q 10 6
◇ 7
♣ K 9 4

Clumsy play from South, but Geir was awake enough to put up his two highest diamonds. If he had not done so declarer would have been more likely to ruff high. Playing the king here was a cost-nothing play for Geir; all it could do was help declarer go wrong.

Deceptive play

At some point in their careers, many bridge players discover the effect of jettisoning an unnecessary high card to fool the opponents about the distribution. Such clever discarding soon becomes a part of top players' normal routine and they do it every time they have the chance, although such trickery can make it easier for declarer, if he reads the cards correctly. Here the play of a deceptive card created total confusion when Geir and three of his regular partners were all at the table.

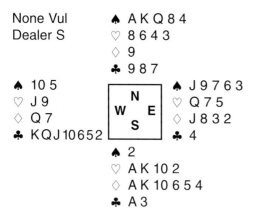

None Vul
Dealer S

```
              ♠ A K Q 8 4
              ♡ 8 6 4 3
              ◇ 9
              ♣ 9 8 7
♠ 10 5                      ♠ J 9 7 6 3
♡ J 9            N          ♡ Q 7 5
◇ Q 7         W   E         ◇ J 8 3 2
♣ K Q J 10 6 5 2    S       ♣ 4
              ♠ 2
              ♡ A K 10 2
              ◇ A K 10 6 5 4
              ♣ A 3
```

The bidding:

West	North	East	South
Helgemo	*Lund*	*Tislevoll*	*Austberg*
—	—	—	1◇
3♣	Dble	Pass	4NT
Pass	5◇	Pass	6♡
All Pass			

Part of Helgemo's early development as a bridge player took place in Heimdal, a suburb just south of Trondheim. Børre Lund is one of the players from the fine bridge club there, and he and Geir learned bridge together. They were also partners for a while, at junior level. Per Erik Austberg had already had some success with Helgemo in tournaments

before they became a real partnership in 1998. They won the 1999 Norwegian Pairs Championship and then Austberg made his international debut in the Bermuda Bowl in January 2000.

This hand occurred in a local tournament in 1996. With these four players at the table a lot of pride was at stake. The slam Lund and Austberg reached was an excellent one, and on seeing all the cards it is hard to see how declarer could go down, but it all happened quite quickly.

The king of clubs was led to the ace, and two spade tricks were cashed to let South discard a club. Then came a diamond to the ace and a diamond ruffed in dummy. The speed of play and declarer's body language told me there was nothing much that could be done to defeat this contract, and I realised that we would get a bad score on the board. But seconds later declarer was one down.

Austberg, generally known as Pil, played a trump to his king. His intention was to cash both the ace and king of trumps, hoping for a 3-2 split, before ruffing another diamond. One trump trick was all the defence would get. But under the first trump honour, the jack fell from West, and South now had something to worry about. The probability of a 4-1 trump break was not that small, but since the jack had appeared, the bad split did not seem a big problem to handle. Pil found the solution, he thought. He could delay cashing his second trump honour, ruff a diamond and play a trump from dummy, finessing his ten of hearts – a safety play. If the finesse failed it did not matter, for the rest of his hand would be high. And if East had four trumps there would still be no problem. One trick in hearts was all that East could get.

Per Erik Austberg

the table. His partner was Per Arne Flått, at the time a good junior player who was on the winning team in the 1990 European Junior Championships.

All Vul   ♠ 6 5 3
Dealer S   ♡ A 10 9 5
           ◇ 8 4
           ♣ 8 7 3 2

```
        N
   W         E
        S
```

    ♠ A K 8
    ♡ 8 6 4
    ◇ A K 7 5
    ♣ A K Q

After a short pause Pil played on diamonds, without cashing his second trump honour. Geir ruffed in with his nine of hearts and continued with a club on which I discarded my last diamond. There was now no entry to dummy to allow declarer to finesse my trump queen. I had been dozing for half of the play on a deal that I had thought was just boring, and was really surprised when Geir ruffed in with his nine. Actually I was so perplexed that I nearly forgot to discard my last diamond when Geir played the club! Fortunately I avoided such a stupid blunder. Pil had to ruff the club and now had no way of avoiding another trump loser.

That was one down in a laydown contract. After the play Pil told me that it was not that painful to go down when it was because of such good defence. As he said: 'This is real bridge !'

In the big Easter teams tournament in Hamar a few years ago Geir found another ingenious way to put pressure on declarer. In fact, the play he found was quite simple, but it was difficult to do at

In the bidding South had shown 23–24 HCP and denied a four-card major suit. Three No-Trumps became the final contract and West led the four of spades. East contributed the ten and South took the first trick with his king. Declarer could see he needed one extra trick in hearts or clubs to make his contract. Therefore he started by cashing his club honours, but West proved to have the jack doubleton when he discarded a spade on the third round of the suit. So declarer had to play for an extra heart trick. If that suit split 3-3 he could duck two hearts and the ace would provide an entry to the North hand on the third round of hearts. He played a heart towards dummy and West put in the jack, which was allowed to hold the trick. Then West played the queen of spades. East produced the seven and South ducked this and took the next spade. Another heart was played: West followed with the two and declarer called for the nine. East produced the king, and cashed the last club, the defence's fourth trick. Then came the jack of diamonds from East and South won. From the start a 3-3 split in hearts was declarer's main chance but, as you may have noticed, the opponents had by now used up two out of the three heart honours. At this moment declarer had these cards left in the critical suit:

♡ A 10

♡ 8

Finesse or not? West has either produced the jack from Q-J-3-2, or he has been very creative by putting up the jack from J-3-2. That latter play would be very unusual, but doing it from the first one, Q-J-3-2, might on some occasions be the correct play. South was in no doubt at all, and he took the finesse. It failed when East produced the queen, and the contract was beaten by two tricks since the ace of hearts was left stranded. It will come as no surprise to you that the player sitting West was Geir Helgemo.

In the previous section I said that most of the top players in Norway, and especially in Trondheim, use straightforward encouraging/discouraging signals. Many players also use suit-preference signals, Smith Peter/Oddball and things like that, but the main pillar of the system is to signal whether you fancy a continuation of the suit played, or not. The rule is that in all situations where partner might need to know whether he should continue a particular suit, or not, we have to tell him what to do. I feel this agreement is good enough, especially for partnerships in Trondheim, who usually do not have the time (or the inclination) to work hard on this, by defining all kinds of specific positions. Geir Helgemo is very easy-going here. He knows that his partners are the ones who will eventually need some kind of convention to help them out, and not him. The simple way of doing things is what he likes best.

Defence should not be based on conventions but on common sense!

When Geir won two Norwegian Pairs Championships in a row with Lasse Aaseng, the kibitzers could see them defend accurately all the time, and most of the time because of common sense. First, an example where the kibitzers had to wonder for a while just what Mr Helgemo was up to:

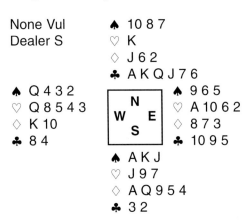

None Vul
Dealer S

♠ 10 8 7
♡ K
♢ J 6 2
♣ A K Q J 7 6

♠ Q 4 3 2
♡ Q 8 5 4 3
♢ K 10
♣ 8 4

♠ 9 6 5
♡ A 10 6 2
♢ 8 7 3
♣ 10 9 5

♠ A K J
♡ J 9 7
♢ A Q 9 5 4
♣ 3 2

The bidding:

West	North	East	South
—	—	—	1NT (1)
Pass	3NT	All Pass	

(1) 15–17

Geir led the three of hearts (3rd & 5th) to the king and Aaseng's ace. Declarer did not like the situation. He and his partner had almost 30 HCP between them, and yet he believed he was likely to go down in his game contract. Of course, this would have to happen against the top pair in the field with a lot of kibitzers around the table. Typical! On the second round of hearts he put in the nine and could breathe again when Helgemo had to take the trick with the queen. The ignominious experience of going down in a mere game with such good cards had been avoided. However, the kibitzers did not really understand when they saw

The long and the short of it – Helgemo with Lasse Aaseng

Geir fail to establish the hearts, and play a club instead. Declarer took the trick and now had time to try the diamond finesse, which failed. Ten tricks. What had really happened here?

The point was that declarer had ten top tricks once he guessed correctly on the second round of hearts. By taking the diamond finesse he was trying for the eleventh trick. It was a free finesse because Geir had not established the hearts. So why did Geir not continue hearts?

The opportunity to take the diamond finesse was given declarer by West, but it was in fact a Greek gift. By counting the high cards Helgemo knew that declarer held all the rest of them, and he could also see that there were ten top tricks. He was essentially playing the hand double-

dummy! The problem for West was that if he established his heart suit he could be quite sure that declarer would never take a finesse in diamonds. He was already so happy that the ten of hearts was onside (since if it had not been, he would have gone down at once) that he would never have taken any chance in his contract. A small pause before his play of the nine of hearts at trick two told Geir that the declarer held the jack. What would have happened if he had established his hearts is that declarer, a competent player, would have played for a spade/diamond squeeze. He would have cashed the ace of diamonds and then run his clubs. The squeeze would work automatically on either defender who held both the king of diamonds and the queen of spades. Geir knew South would make eleven tricks so he gave him a chance to lose one more trick, and he did so. The score sheet proved that the defence had actually worked out well. About half of the North/South pairs played Three No-Trumps making five, plus 460. Minus 430 gave Aaseng and Helgemo a 69% score on the board.

Here is another deal from the Pairs Championship:

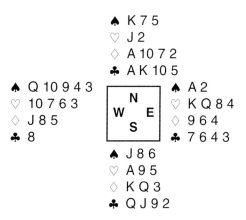

♠ K 7 5
♡ J 2
♢ A 10 7 2
♣ A K 10 5

♠ Q 10 9 4 3
♡ 10 7 6 3
♢ J 8 5
♣ 8

♠ A 2
♡ K Q 8 4
♢ 9 6 4
♣ 7 6 4 3

♠ J 8 6
♡ A 9 5
♢ K Q 3
♣ Q J 9 2

Once again the bidding went 1NT – 3NT, but this time the opening showed 13–15

Repeated
for
convenience

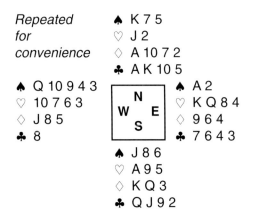

♠ K 7 5
♡ J 2
◇ A 10 7 2
♣ A K 10 5

♠ Q 10 9 4 3
♡ 10 7 6 3
◇ J 8 5
♣ 8

♠ A 2
♡ K Q 8 4
◇ 9 6 4
♣ 7 6 4 3

♠ J 8 6
♡ A 9 5
◇ K Q 3
♣ Q J 9 2

HCP. Geir led the three of spades (3rd & 5th). When declarer played low from dummy Aaseng put up his ace and switched to the king of hearts. In this situation we Norwegians use encouraging/discouraging signals. By counting the high cards both defenders know that declarer must hold the ace, so usually West will encourage if he holds the ten. Some people play count in this type of situation. They argue that it is obvious if declarer has the ten or not, because if South holds the ten he will always cover the king with his ace. That is usually true, but in our opinion it is still better to play encouraging/discouraging. The message from West to East is not whether he holds the ten or not, but if he wants a continuation or not. To encourage does not mean that a particular card is held, it simply tells partner that a continuation looks best from that side of the table. Conversely, discouragement does not deny the ten in this situation. It just tells partner that it does not look so good to continue the suit. Now just watch the developments:

Although the Norwegian style is to use small cards to encourage, at the second trick Helgemo surprisingly played his seven of hearts, discouraging! An obedient Aaseng

switched back to spades to the eight, ten and king. Later declarer took eight top tricks in the minors and his heart ace, a total of ten tricks. What was so special about this?

Well, Helgemo's discouraging seven of hearts was not an accident. Look what happens if he encourages: Aaseng will then continue with the queen of hearts to declarer's ace. South takes his four diamond tricks and discards the eight of spades on the last one. Then he runs the clubs, and this is the position:

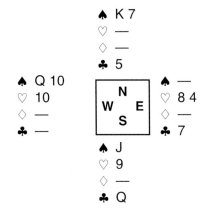

♠ K 7
♡ —
◇ —
♣ 5

♠ Q 10
♡ 10
◇ —
♣ —

♠ —
♡ 8 4
◇ —
♣ 7

♠ J
♡ 9
◇ —
♣ Q

On the last club West is caught in a simple squeeze. Everyone has to reduce to two cards. East has hearts, but his eight is not high enough, so West needs to guard the heart suit and cannot also keep spades.

A heart lead would have held declarer to nine tricks this time, but the spade lead was quite normal. Only a few declarers were held to nine tricks in the big pairs final. Some players made eleven on the squeeze, so Helgemo's ability to foresee the development when his partner played the king of hearts produced a bushel of extra points. Eleven tricks would have given East/West only an 8% score, while minus 430 gave them a little over average. So it pays to be farsighted.

Part Six

Brilliancy

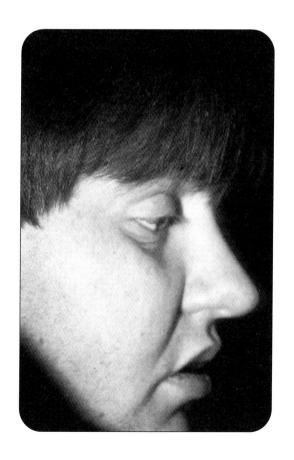

The stroke of genius

After declarer has missed a complex line of play, you often hear him say: 'I should have followed my first instincts'.

Or: 'The first thing I thought of was right, as always…'

But there are no consolation prizes, and the only one who believes your excuse will be you! In bridge the stroke of genius often comes too late, but you would like to think that it was at least in there all the time. For the same reason many bridge players sometimes say: 'That play was not so difficult!', and: 'What else could he have done?' when hearing about somebody's good play. They forget that it is so much more difficult at the table.

Helgemo is a player who sometimes formulates his play even before he has seen dummy, and may make his plan for the play before the bidding has finished. When it comes to moving fast he has surprised me many times. As declarer or defender, he sometimes produces a series of small manoeuvres that I often need to think about for hours before I understand what was in his mind. Often the other players never work out the reason for his actions at the table, because the manoeuvre he executed did not generate an extra trick – that time – but it could have done so if the cards had been different. He gives himself extra chances all the time.

Helgemo is not the type of guy who tells everybody about his good plays – showing off is not his style. That is why many of his master strokes are born to blush unseen.

Many players feel Helgemo is extremely lucky. Often people say things like: 'He is a good player, but he is also incredibly lucky.'

You often see the opponents take their ten top tricks against you, but when you talk to Helgemo, you discover that his opponents have gone down in their major-suit game. Where did he find the setting trick? Shaking your head, you return to your own world. It seems as if they just do not want to take their tricks against that man!

Often the truth is that Geir made some clever play which gave the poor declarer an awkward choice.

'It costs nothing to give them enough rope to hang themselves,' he likes to say.

This chapter details hands that have won Geir Helgemo brilliancy prizes, and a few plays that deserved a prize but turned up in tournaments where no such prizes were awarded. Some of the hands are well known, but they are so extraordinary that they certainly bear repeating. Other hands have never been published before.

Such hands sometimes contain a beautiful technical point, but quite often the real problem is simply to think of the idea in the first place.

The first hand in this category received no prize. It was played in a small, local pairs tournament in Trøndelag, and was forgotten for some years. As far as I know it has never been published before. I was the astonished spectator sitting North.

NS Vul
Dealer W

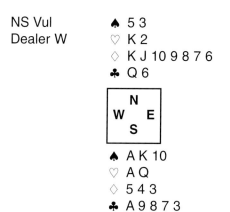

♠ 5 3
♡ K 2
◇ K J 10 9 8 7 6
♣ Q 6

♠ A K 10
♡ A Q
◇ 5 4 3
♣ A 9 8 7 3

West passed and I opened Three Diamonds. East passed and Geir bid the obvious Three No-Trumps. West led the queen of spades. East discouraged and Geir took the trick with his ace. Then he led a diamond towards dummy. It looked as if he might be confronted with an awkward guess, but this time it was easy since West played his queen on the first round of the suit. This was the full layout:

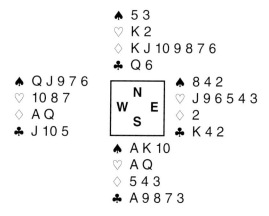

♠ 5 3
♡ K 2
◇ K J 10 9 8 7 6
♣ Q 6

♠ Q J 9 7 6   ♠ 8 4 2
♡ 10 8 7   ♡ J 9 6 5 4 3
◇ A Q   ◇ 2
♣ J 10 5   ♣ K 4 2

♠ A K 10
♡ A Q
◇ 5 4 3
♣ A 9 8 7 3

You may wonder what kind of brilliancy prize hand this was? It looks as if there are eleven tricks on top, does it not? Well, the daring play Helgemo found is yet to come, and it is difficult to see even with the sight of all 52 cards. On the second round of diamonds West got in and switched to a heart.

All the other declarers were in the same position and happily took their

eleven tricks for 660, while Geir paused for some seconds. Then he put up the king of hearts. Next, as if it was the most obvious play in the world, he called for the queen of clubs! East had to cover; if he had not done so the queen would have been allowed to ride, and would have produced the twelfth trick. The ace of clubs captured East's king. Then the ace of hearts was cashed and it was time to run the diamonds. Before the last one this was the ending:

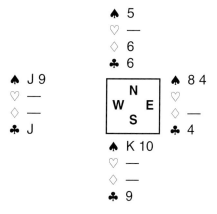

♠ 5
♡ —
◇ 6
♣ 6

♠ J 9   ♠ 8 4
♡ —   ♡
◇ —   ◇ —
♣ J   ♣ 4

♠ K 10
♡ —
◇ —
♣ 9

The six of diamonds was played. South threw his nine of clubs, and it was up to West to find a discard. Dummy's six of clubs had become a perfect threat against West, and he could do nothing but throw in the towel. Twelve tricks made on the squeeze produced a top, of course.

On the last hand the squeeze had to be in spades and clubs. The card threatening West in spades was South's ten, so according to the squeeze theories, one menace has to be placed behind the player who is to be squeezed, in this case West. So the menace in clubs had to be in North's hand.

The easiest way of getting a squeeze of this type to work is to take the ace of clubs and then squeeze West if he holds the king of clubs in addition to the spade stopper which he has already revealed. But that line would not have worked this time.

West's holding the king of clubs is much more likely than his holding both the jack and the ten, which was what Geir needed to make his play work.

So why did he play like that? The point was that West had passed in first seat, and had already shown the Q-J of spades and A-Q of diamonds. If he also held the king of clubs, that would be a total of 12 HCP. With a spade suit and 12 HCP 'everyone' opens, especially not vulnerable. That meant Geir knew where the king of clubs was, and he could go for the spectacular play, which left West as the only one with a club stopper.

The idea of transferring a stopper from one opponent to the other, who is later to be squeezed, is a well-known technique. If dummy's clubs had been Q-10 doubleton the hand would have been close to a textbook example. With such a club holding it would be far easier to have the flash of inspiration to play the queen from dummy, transferring the stopper from East's king to West's jack, and then squeezing West in spades and clubs. But here, since the menace in clubs had to be dummy's six, East could not hold the jack or the ten in addition to his king. The problem for declarer was to visualise such a club distribution and then to play the queen from dummy.

Being a flexible partner has always been one of Helgemo's strengths, a quality he needed when participating for the first time in the Generali Masters (the World Individual Championship) in 1996. In a tournament of that type it is not enough to be one of the best players in the world. Being able to adapt to playing with different partners is vital. The tournament turned into a personal triumph for Geir Helgemo, and he won his second world title.

On this hand he found a play that eluded everyone else.

None Vul	♠ A Q 9
Dealer S	♡ 10 8 4 3
	◇ 4 3 2
	♣ A K 6

```
        N
    W       E
        S
```

♠ K 5
♡ Q J 6
◇ A K 7
♣ 9 8 4 3 2

The bidding:

West	North	East	South
—	—	—	1♣
Pass	1♡	Pass	1NT
Pass	3NT	All Pass	

His opponents were Berry Westra (Netherlands) and Dick Freeman (USA). Geir, who was partnering Hervé Mouiel (France), was declarer in Three No-Trumps, and Westra led the queen of diamonds. At all the other tables declarer led a low club immediately, winning with

Berry Westra

dummy's ace when West contributed the five. To be honest, extreme farsightedness is needed to find any extra chance. But, by contrast with all the other Souths, on the first round of clubs Geir played the eight from his hand. That really hit the bull's eye when the whole hand looked like this:

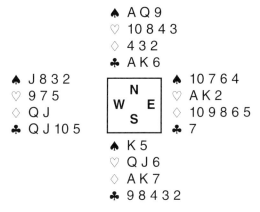

Dick Freeman

West could do nothing but admire South's play. If he covered the eight with one of his high clubs, he would see his partner's singleton seven fall under the ace. Declarer could later play another club towards dummy, finessing the six if West did not put up an honour again! West's nice double stopper had been transformed into only one trick. In practice West played small on the eight, which was allowed to ride and took the trick. Again, the main problem was to latch on to the idea in the first place!

It was possible to make Three No-Trumps in other ways because of the red-suit situation. Taking nine tricks for a plus score of 400 scored only average. However, when Geir's eight of clubs had held the trick he could turn his attention to hearts. Thus he was eventually able to take ten tricks for a top, scoring a bushel of valuable matchpoints on his way to the world title.

When the small cards start to grow

Most of the hands in this book feature Geir Helgemo as a player, but he is also a good columnist in Norway's biggest newspaper, *VG* (*Verdens Gang*). In his columns, and in bulletins during championships, he often writes articles about his friends and his opponents. Some of them have earned him press awards, although most of the awards he has received have been as a player.

From time to time Geir has written about me. When I have been involved in an interesting hand but not solved the problem, he doesn't always mention my name. But if I have had one of my bright moments he always tells the readers who did it!

This first hand happened at the big summer festival in Kristiansand. I could have been the hero, but unfortunately ended up with egg on my face. Can you see what I should have done?

```
NS Vul          ♠ A J 5
Dealer S        ♡ Q 9 5
                ◇ Q J 4 3
                ♣ A 10 3
              ┌─────────┐
              │    N    │
              │  W   E  │
              │    S    │
              └─────────┘
                ♠ Q 10 9 8 6
                ♡ K J 6
                ◇ 8 5 2
                ♣ K Q
```

The bidding:

West	North	East	South
—	—	—	1♠
Pass	2◇	Dble	2NT
Pass	3NT	All Pass	

I was South and needed to bring home this game contract. West led the eight of hearts which was taken in hand, East playing a small, encouraging, card. Next came the queen of spades which was allowed to hold the trick. Another spade was played to the jack, but East showed out. Then the ace of spades. What now?

The problem was that even though there are nine tricks on top it is not so easy to take them all. If South cashes both his club honours before clearing the spades West may play another club when in with his king of spades, and declarer will be dead. If only one club is cashed before playing on spades the defence clear the hearts and declarer cannot get to his third club trick in dummy. Or … ? I felt I had seen the position before. Then I had a bright thought and saw the light. A stepping-stone squeeze!

It was quite likely the original layout was something like this:

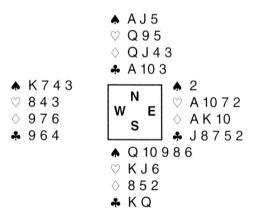

```
                ♠ A J 5
                ♡ Q 9 5
                ◇ Q J 4 3
                ♣ A 10 3
  ♠ K 7 4 3   ┌───────┐   ♠ 2
  ♡ 8 4 3     │   N   │   ♡ A 10 7 2
  ◇ 9 7 6     │ W   E │   ◇ A K 10
  ♣ 9 6 4     │   S   │   ♣ J 8 7 5 2
              └───────┘
                ♠ Q 10 9 8 6
                ♡ K J 6
                ◇ 8 5 2
                ♣ K Q
```

After two spade finesses and the ace of spades I played a club to the queen. Then another spade. West won and played a heart to East's ace and he played a third round of the suit. This was left:

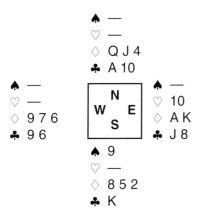

The nine of spades was played and a diamond thrown from dummy. East couldn't find a good discard. If he threw a diamond honour he would make only two more tricks. If he threw the heart I could cash my last club and play a diamond, and East would have to help me reach the table. And finally, if he threw a club I could play the king overtaking with the ace dropping the jack! I must admit I was very pleased about spotting this play on one of the last rounds … but I was just a little too quick. East threw a club on the eight of spades and I triumphantly played the king of clubs asking for the ace from dummy. But East followed with the seven instead of the supposed jack!

What had gone wrong? One down, everybody said, but I couldn't accept that. It was my stepping-stone squeeze, come on folks! But, no – one down, they insisted. Then I understood what had happened. I haven't told you yet what East discarded on the early rounds of spades. At trick four, when I cashed the ace of spades, East threw his ten of diamonds. But at trick three, he had thrown his fourth heart! And I hadn't seen it! My opponent had at trick three done what he was supposed to do at trick nine. My face soon turned a nice shade of red.

Happily I had another opportunity to win the Best Played Hand award in Kristiansand. But, as Helgemo said: 'You would not have won that award if your bidding hadn't been so lousy.'

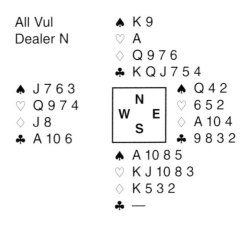

All Vul
Dealer N

The bidding:

West	North	East	South
—	1♣	Pass	1♡
Pass	2♣	Pass	2♢ (1)
Pass	3♢	Pass	5♢
All Pass			

(1) just forcing, not showing diamonds

My Five Diamond bid was rather hasty. Over the alternative Three Spades, partner would have tried Three No-Trumps which is a better contract.

The lead from West was the six of spades (3rd & 5th). I took it with the king and played the king of clubs. The best chance is to find the ace with East, and ruff it out. If West wins the club, as he does here, Five Diamonds depends on finding the trump ace doubleton. As you can see, this does not work as the cards lie. East played a small club smoothly on the king so I was quite sure he didn't have the ace. As I didn't want to give up, I changed tack and played for something else. The king of clubs was ruffed, then a heart to the ace was followed by another club ruff. Next came the king of hearts with a club discard from dummy and then a heart ruff. A third club was ruffed in hand, West playing the ace. Now the ace of spades was cashed and a spade ruffed in dummy. This was the delicate end-position, with me needing two more tricks:

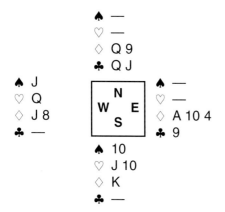

Now came a good club from dummy, and East had to follow. To make my contract I had to ruff with the singleton trump king. West was caught in the opposite of a squeeze – he wanted to discard *both* his major-suit cards on this trick! In practice, he discarded a spade, and now I played a heart. West had to follow and I now just discarded a club from dummy. East, who had only trumps left, had to ruff and concede a trump trick to dummy's queen, the eleventh trick.

The 2000 Bermuda Bowl saw the appearance at international level of a new partnership, that of Helgemo and Per Erik Austberg, although Geir still played with Tor Helness for some of the time. It seemed as if the Norwegian team would be stronger with its two stars in different partnerships.

Tor Helness is the most experienced player on the Norwegian team. He is only 43 years old, but has been playing internationally since the late seventies.

Tor and I were both on the team that won the Junior European Championship in 1980. At that point he was one of the best players in Norway, and already established as a member of the Norwegian open team. I am sure Tor will be the anchor of Norway's team for many more years, and he and Helgemo will soon help bring home Norway's first ever world team championship title.

Helness is known as a steady player who seldom makes mistakes. His play is accurate, and he is also a great analyst of the hands. Compared with Helgemo, Tor is more of a mechanical player, who does not try so many spectacular coups. But he has also made many great plays, and won many brilliancy prizes. Once he received the Best Played Hand award in the Norwegian Championship. The reporter was Helgemo, who for once had not qualified for the tournament, but instead he won the press prize. Here it is, a really fine piece of work:

None Vul
Dealer S

♠ 5 2
♡ J 7 5 4
♢ 7 5
♣ K Q J 7 6

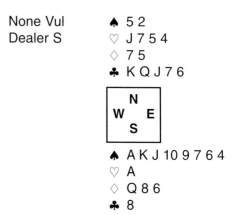

♠ A K J 10 9 7 6 4
♡ A
♢ Q 8 6
♣ 8

The bidding:

West	North	East	South
—	—	—	1♠
Pass	1NT	Dble	4♠
Dble	All Pass		

Try it yourself. West leads the nine of clubs to the jack and ace. East switches to the eight of spades. Make a plan before looking below.

Dummy's resources were not what you were hoping for when you jumped to Four Spades. There are no entries to dummy's clubs so it looks as if you will lose three diamond tricks in addition to the club trick you have already lost. This was how the full hand looked:

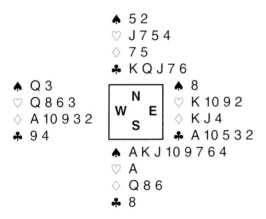

Did you manage to take the finesse in trumps and create a trump loser? Look at the position from West's point of view. It is not so easy for him to realise that declarer has taken the finesse with eight such good spades opposite a doubleton. So West continued trumps, but dummy's five was big enough to be an entry. Two good clubs provided discards for two diamonds and ten tricks were made.

I have already mentioned the Bridge Festival in Tel Aviv in 1996 where I went instead of Helness. One of the most fascinating boards of the whole week was this one, with Geir in the driving seat:

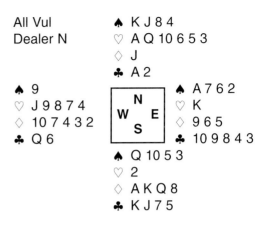

```
All Vul          ♠ K J 8 4
Dealer N         ♡ A Q 10 6 5 3
                 ◇ J
                 ♣ A 2
```

The bidding:

West	North	East	South
	Tislevoll		*Helgemo*
—	1♡	Pass	1♠
Pass	3♠	Pass	4♣
Pass	4◇	Pass	4♡
Pass	4NT	Pass	5◇
Pass	5♡	Pass	6◇
Pass	6♠	All Pass	

Our opponents were a top-level German team, and the match against them came when the tournament was starting to reach its climax.

The first three bids were natural. Then came a few cue-bids followed by Four No-Trumps, Roman Key Card Blackwood. North could identify that one ace was missing so the slam would be too challenging without the trump queen. Therefore he tried Five Hearts, asking for the trump queen. Six Diamonds showed both the queen of trumps and the king of diamonds.

Against the slam West led the queen of clubs, an imaginative but unlucky lead. It was a good start for declarer, but even so, twelve tricks were still not easy: the trumps do not break, the king of hearts is offside, and there are terrible communication problems. Geir paused before he started playing, so I knew the slam was far from laydown. The ace of

Repeated
for
convenience

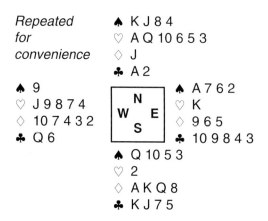

♠ K J 8 4
♡ A Q 10 6 5 3
◇ J
♣ A 2

♠ 9
♡ J 9 8 7 4
◇ 10 7 4 3 2
♣ Q 6

♠ A 7 6 2
♡ K
◇ 9 6 5
♣ 10 9 8 4 3

♠ Q 10 5 3
♡ 2
◇ A K Q 8
♣ K J 7 5

clubs took the first trick. Then Geir played the jack of spades, which was allowed to hold, followed by a spade to the queen, which also held. A third round of trumps went to the king and ace. On the second and third round of trumps West discarded a diamond and a heart. Clearly, now a trump would have been best, but East played the four of clubs. Geir went up with the king of clubs, and ruffed the seven of clubs with dummy's last trump, on which West had to throw another heart. This was left:

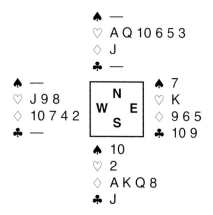

♠ —
♡ A Q 10 6 5 3
◇ J
♣ —

♠ —
♡ J 9 8
◇ 10 7 4 2
♣ —

♠ 7
♡ K
◇ 9 6 5
♣ 10 9

♠ 10
♡ 2
◇ A K Q 8
♣ J

Declarer has the rest in top tricks, but how can he get to them? As mentioned

earlier in the play, there were terrible communication problems, and the play still looks difficult. Geir played the jack of diamonds and overtook it with the ace. He had now lost one of his top winners, but that did not seem to bother him much. When he led out his last trump, East's last trump was drawn. Then the two remaining diamond tricks were cashed, and when the jack of clubs was played, the position was like a textbook example:

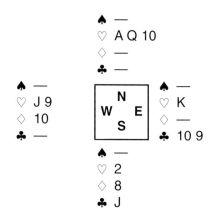

♠ —
♡ A Q 10
◇ —
♣ —

♠ —
♡ J 9
◇ 10
♣ —

♠ —
♡ K
◇ —
♣ 10 9

♠ —
♡ 2
◇ 8
♣ J

West had to keep his ten of diamonds and therefore had to reduce to only one heart. The location of the king of hearts was academic. The suit had to be 1-1 in the end-position, since East was known to have held two clubs and a heart in the three-card ending. He could, of course, have started life with four diamonds and a void in hearts, but that was not likely since he did not make a Lightner double of the slam, demanding a heart lead which he could have ruffed. When Geir played a heart to the ace in the ending I could dry my sweaty face and breathe again. By contrast, Geir looked as if he had just finished an everyday hand.

Helgemo's finesse

In the 1988 European Junior Championships in Plovdiv, Bulgaria, the Welshman Patrick Jourdain told the bulletin readers about the 18-year-old Geir Helgemo from Norway. International bridge journalists had already discovered the extraordinary new talent. They followed him closely and soon got the story they wanted.

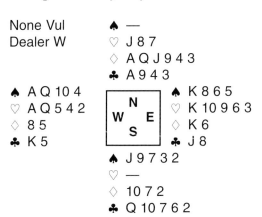

None Vul
Dealer W

	♠ —	
	♡ J 8 7	
	◇ A Q J 9 4 3	
	♣ A 9 4 3	
♠ A Q 10 4		♠ K 8 6 5
♡ A Q 5 4 2	N	♡ K 10 9 6 3
◇ 8 5	W E	◇ K 6
♣ K 5	S	♣ J 8
	♠ J 9 7 3 2	
	♡ —	
	◇ 10 7 2	
	♣ Q 10 7 6 2	

Tom Johansen

West	North	East	South
1♡	2◇	4♡	Pass
Pass	4NT	Pass	5♣
Dble	All Pass		

Four Hearts will make for East/West provided West is declarer. If North/South sacrifice in Five Diamonds and push their opponents to Five Hearts that contract will go one down on careful defence. The Norwegians playing East/West in the Closed Room avoided bidding on to Five Hearts, but defending against the doubled sacrifice of Five Diamonds worked out considerably worse, since nothing could be done to beat that contract.

The Norwegian spectators in the VuGraph could only hope that the Norwegian pair in the Open Room would flatten that result, and that East/West would not bid Five Hearts, which in fact turned out to be the real sacrifice on the hand.

With Tom Johansen playing North and Geir Helgemo South the bidding went:

Good bidding by Johansen. With his three-card heart suit he knew his partner had at most one heart, so there had to be good prospects for a minor-suit contract for North/South. But it was not certain that South would hold diamond support, so Four No-Trumps was the most flexible bid, showing a four-card club suit. (With five clubs North would bid Five Clubs himself, or he would have bid Two No-Trumps, the unusual no-trump, on the previous round.)

Unfortunately the club game was more challenging than the diamond game, especially because West found the incisive lead of the ace of spades. Geir ruffed in dummy, ruffed a heart and took a losing diamond finesse. The spade continuation put further pressure on declarer. He ruffed again, and this was the position:

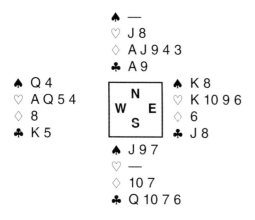

```
                ♠ —
                ♡ J 8
                ◇ A J 9 4 3
                ♣ A 9
  ♠ Q 4                        ♠ K 8
  ♡ A Q 5 4      N             ♡ K 10 9 6
  ◇ 8         W     E          ◇ 6
  ♣ K 5          S             ♣ J 8
                ♠ J 9 7
                ♡ —
                ◇ 10 7
                ♣ Q 10 7 6
```

This was good defence. Declarer needs to let the opponents make their trump trick before he can discard spade losers on the diamonds. But then there is the danger that the defenders will cash their spade tricks. The Norwegian supporters began to fear a big loss on the board. However, the play was soon finished and plus 550 written on the score sheet. In the diagrammed situation Geir played the nine of clubs from dummy and let it run to West's king. The defence did its best by pressing on with more spades, but declarer ruffed with the trump ace before ruffing a heart to hand. Then the rest of the trumps were drawn with the queen.

Patrick Jourdain named this play 'the Helgemo finesse', a name that would be revived some years later.

Geir Helgemo and Tor Helness won the 1999 Romex Award for the Best Auction for the Seven Diamonds they bid in the 1999 Macallan Tournament (see page 47). Patrick Jourdain wrote the article that brought the hand to light. Here Patrick and Geir receive their awards.

In tempo

Geir Helgemo has always been very successful in mixed pairs tournaments and has put together many fine results together with different female players in Norway. For instance, he won the Norwegian Mixed Championship with Signy Johansen, who also partnered Geir when this lovely deal occurred in the big summer tournament in Kristiansand in 1998.

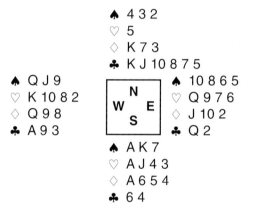

They were playing matchpoints. A normal bidding sequence was for North to raise his partner's One No-Trump opening to game. If South had had a club honour, North could see that Three No-Trumps would have been a very good contract. As it was, the contract was not hopeless.

On a heart lead the contract is doomed – the defence will take three heart tricks and two clubs. But at some tables West led the queen of spades. Then, to beat the contract East had to find the heart switch before the clubs were set up. If he did not, the defence would get only two spade tricks and two clubs. Signy led the queen of spades. Do you think Geir found the heart switch? Well, he did not have to, since the contract had to go two down anyway!

When declarer at trick two played a club to dummy's jack, the finesse worked! Geir kept his queen of clubs for later use, instead following with the two. Naturally declarer went wrong. He played a diamond to the ace and continued his attack on clubs. Signy followed with a small card again, and again declarer finessed, but this time, to his surprise, the ten lost to the queen. Declarer was later able to develop an extra diamond trick, but could not come to more than seven tricks, for a bottom on the board.

Signy with Helgemo

Experience

The best players develop habits that do not produce extra tricks on every single occasion. These are plays that they can make without cost, where it does not matter that on a given day the play does not produce a dividend – eventually such a play will be rewarded.

This board is from a knockout match in the 1996 Norwegian Teams Championship.

```
All Vul          ♠ K 8 5
Dealer S         ♡ K 6 5
                 ◇ A 7 3
                 ♣ J 10 7 2

              N
           W     E
              S

                 ♠ A 10 7 6 4 2
                 ♡ A Q J
                 ◇ 8
                 ♣ A K Q
```

The bidding:

West	North	East	South
—	—	—	1♠
Pass	3♠	Pass	4NT
Pass	5♡	Pass	6♠
All Pass			

The bidding was not especially scientific. My bid of Three Spades would normally show four-card support, but the opening promised a five-card suit, and nothing else appealed. Four No-Trumps was Roman Key Card Blackwood and Five Hearts showed two aces out of five, including the trump king. Six Spades was a good contract; indeed, if I had had a fourth trump the grand would have been excellent.

The queen of diamonds was led to dummy's ace, and a small diamond immediately ruffed in hand. That is a typical expert move: ruffing a loser early to start the process of shortening trumps, just in case. Such a play should be routine. A bad trump break is the only thing that can create problems for declarer. Next Geir played a spade towards dummy, intending to finesse the eight to guard against all four trumps with West. If West shows out on the first round there will be no problems on the deal, as declarer can pick up trumps by playing the king and another spade, and East cannot get more than one trump trick. But this time West held all the trumps. He was looking at two secure trump tricks and did not want to allow Geir to take the deep finesse, so he put in the nine, forcing declarer to put up the king. East discarded a diamond. This was how the full deal looked:

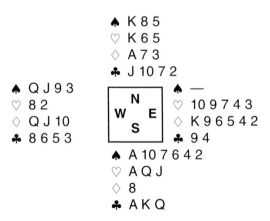

```
              ♠ K 8 5
              ♡ K 6 5
              ◇ A 7 3
              ♣ J 10 7 2
♠ Q J 9 3              ♠ —
♡ 8 2          N      ♡ 10 9 7 4 3
◇ Q J 10    W    E    ◇ K 9 6 5 4 2
♣ 8 6 5 3      S      ♣ 9 4
              ♠ A 10 7 6 4 2
              ♡ A Q J
              ◇ 8
              ♣ A K Q
```

When West put in the nine he thought he had ensured his two trump tricks, but they were not such sure winners after all. From declarer's viewpoint, it looked as if West would have to follow suit three times in both clubs and hearts if an endplay in trumps was going to work.

However, if West had four clubs, the endplay would also work, so Geir played clubs first. Since East followed suit only twice, it was clear that West would later have to follow to a fourth round of clubs also, thus only two rounds of hearts needed to stand up. The queen of hearts was played, and next the jack of hearts went to dummy's king. This was left:

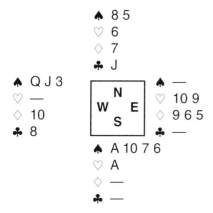

```
              ♠ 8 5
              ♡ 6
              ◇ 7
              ♣ J
  ♠ Q J 3          ♠ —
  ♡ —      N       ♡ 10 9
  ◇ 10   W   E     ◇ 9 6 5
  ♣ 8      S       ♣ —
              ♠ A 10 7 6
              ♡ A
              ◇ —
              ♣ —
```

Look how West has been gradually 'stripped' of his plain cards. In the diagrammed position declarer was in dummy, and the jack of clubs was played, discarding the ace of hearts. Then came the last diamond, ruffed in hand. With only three cards left, both West and South held only trumps. A small trump from South let West take one trick with his jack, but then he had to lead into declarer's A-10 and concede the contract.

If West had instead been dealt three hearts and a doubleton diamond, it would have been necessary to follow another line to make the hand. Declarer would have had to cash three hearts, and then shorten his own trumps by ruffing the fourth club. After cashing the third heart (before reaching the diagram above) he could ruff the jack of clubs in hand, and the ending would then be the same. The choice between these two plays was something of a guess, although the percentages favour West holding three cards in diamonds not hearts, since you have only four diamonds between your two hands, as opposed to six hearts.

Geir so often succeeds in this kind of pretty play not only because of his good card-playing technique, but also because he usually chooses the right alternative when there is little to go on. Plus 1430 was for him a normal result on these cards. It is good to be his partner then, but not so much fun to be an opponent…

Geo and Geir

Killing defence

A defence produced by Helgemo in 1998 was given the Best Defence Award of the year by IBPA (the International Bridge Press Association). The defence included two advanced coups, with the same card! The first is called the Deschappelles Coup, which occurs when a defender plays an unsupported honour to create an entry for his partner. The Merrimac Coup takes place when a player sacrifices his unsupported honour to dislodge a vital entry to one of declarer's hands, usually the dummy. Geir did both on the same trick! Here is the masterpiece:

Paul Chemla

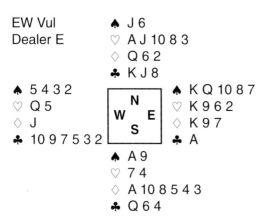

```
EW Vul          ♠ J 6
Dealer E        ♡ A J 10 8 3
                ◇ Q 6 2
                ♣ K J 8
♠ 5 4 3 2              ♠ K Q 10 8 7
♡ Q 5           N      ♡ K 9 6 2
◇ J          W     E   ◇ K 9 7
♣ 10 9 7 5 3 2   S     ♣ A
                ♠ A 9
                ♡ 7 4
                ◇ A 10 8 5 4 3
                ♣ Q 6 4
```

The bidding:

West	North	East	South
—	—	1♠	2◇
Pass	2♡	Pass	3◇
3♠	4◇	All Pass	

This happened in the Generali Masters where there were bridge celebrities from all around the world at every table. Geir was East and opened the bidding. It was maybe a little strange that West did not support spades on the first round, but that did not matter, since North/South were pushed to Four Diamonds anyway.

East/West can make eight or nine tricks in a spade contract, but no more if the defence is accurate. South was Dick Freeman from the USA and North Paul Chemla from France.

Against Four Diamonds Geir's partner led a low spade to the ten and ace. Declarer continued spades and Geir was in with his queen. His next move was not so easy to find at the table; he cashed his ace of clubs before playing the king of hearts!

The defence is not impossible to spot with the sight of all four hands, but remember Geir could see only his own cards and dummy's. Now declarer could not make his contract any more, even though trumps behaved well. He took the trick with dummy's ace of hearts and played the queen of diamonds. East covered with the king, and the jack fell under the ace. Now declarer tried to get to dummy in clubs, but that was not a good idea. Geir ruffed, played a heart to his partner and got a second club ruff for two down.

Another defence that got a lot of coverage in the newspapers all over the world was the hand recounted below. This exciting defence happened in the 1996 World Teams Olympiad:

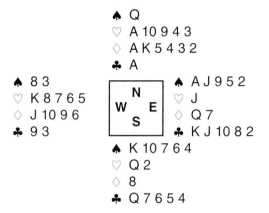

East, Tor Helness, had bid his spades before South became declarer in Three No-Trumps. Geir led his eight of spades to the queen and East took the ace. He switched to a low club. In such situations Tor and Geir play attitude: a small card promises something useful in the suit led. Geir played his nine, discouraging, and dummy's ace won the trick. Then declarer went after the diamonds, playing ace, king and another. Geir took the third diamond.

Now came a most spectacular killing switch: the king of hearts! It killed declarer's communications and the contract was doomed. When the smoke had cleared declarer had gone two down; a well-deserved result for the Norwegians since on many defences declarer could easily end up with nine tricks.

Many bridge journalists claimed in their columns that declarer also would go down if West played a low heart, but they said Geir's beautiful switch – the king of hearts – also catered for the possibility that declarer held the king of clubs. But in truth if Geir had switched to a low heart, declarer can succeed even without the king of clubs. Let's see what happens if West plays a low heart, which goes to the jack and queen. Now, if he reads the cards correctly, declarer must play a low club from his hand. East must take the trick and he has to give declarer one trick in either spades or clubs. The most probable development is that East would play the king of clubs and a club to South's queen. On those two rounds of clubs West has to discard twice, and he throws a heart and the three of spades. This would then have been the position:

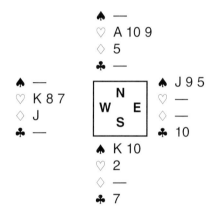

South has five tricks and he can easily take three more, the king of spades and two heart tricks with a finesse through West. However, when he cashes his king of spades, West has to keep his diamond and when he throws a heart declarer takes three more tricks in that suit, for a total of nine.

This line of play would have been easier for declarer if he had held the king or queen-jack of clubs, but it only works if West switches to a low heart. Once he chose the king instead, declarer had no chance at all.

Another finesse

During the 1997 US Spring Nationals Geir had the honour of playing on the same team as the legendary Edgar Kaplan who died the same year. In spite of his serious illness, Kaplan played good bridge, and his team won the tournament. That was Helgemo's first American title.

In one of the matches Kaplan partnered Helgemo, who then found one of the most spectacular plays in the history of bridge. Many readers will have seen the hand before, but it is so beautiful that it should certainly be reported again.

None Vul
Dealer W

♠ 9 7 3
♡ 9 7 6 2
◇ K 10 8 6
♣ 9 2

♠ A K 6 2
♡ —
◇ A Q J 9 7 4 2
♣ A 8

The bidding:

West	North	East	South
	Kaplan		Helgemo
2♡	Pass	4♡	6◇
All Pass			

West's Two Heart opening was weak. When it was Geir's turn to speak he bid what he thought he could make, namely an optimistic slam – practical bidding at its best.

Although Kaplan was a helpful partner and held a little more than Helgemo could have expected, he held one spade too many. The contract was clearly going to be tough to make.

Edgar Kaplan

The king of hearts was led and Geir ruffed. He had two possible losers, one in each of the black suits. There was a spade loser for sure, so he needed to make three spade tricks to get a discard for his club loser. Can you see any possibilities besides the obvious one, of a 3-3 split in spades? Geir Helgemo managed to envisage a situation in spades that could give him three spade tricks even if the suit was 4-2. The possible layout was:

♠ 8 x   ♠ Q J 10 x

Even when you see it set out like this, it may be difficult to realise how Geir could make three tricks against this lie of the cards. But in practice the play was over in seconds. After drawing the trumps (they were 1-1) Geir played the two of spades towards dummy. West played the four and Geir took the finesse, by playing the seven from dummy. East produced the jack before continuing with the five of spades. Without hesitation Geir played small and took the trick with dummy's nine since West could not produce anything bigger than the eight! This was the full layout:

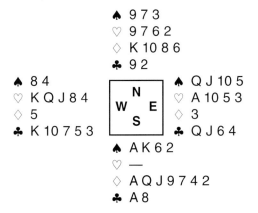

```
              ♠ 9 7 3
              ♡ 9 7 6 2
              ◇ K 10 8 6
              ♣ 9 2
  ♠ 8 4                      ♠ Q J 10 5
  ♡ K Q J 8 4      N         ♡ A 10 5 3
  ◇ 5          W       E     ◇ 3
  ♣ K 10 7 5 3      S        ♣ Q J 6 4
              ♠ A K 6 2
              ♡ —
              ◇ A Q J 9 7 4 2
              ♣ A 8
```

This play is extraordinary. Let's have a look at the spades once more:

```
              ♠ 9 7 3
  ♠ 8 4                  ♠ Q J 10 5
              ♠ A K 6 2
```

The suit had to provide three tricks, and South started by leading the two of spades towards dummy. When West played the four Geir finessed – the first finesse – playing dummy's seven. It forced out one of East's big spades. He continued with the five and Geir let it go to the nine. It was certainly not impossible that West held three spades, but that is where Geir's table presence came into play. The point was that West, on the first round of the suit, followed with his smallest spade with no pause at all. Maybe he would have taken the trick if he had held the ten, for instance? Or

perhaps he would at least have paused briefly? If East had not continued spades, Geir would have played a trump to dummy and called for the nine of spades, intending to take a second finesse in the suit. Whether East covers or not does not matter. Let us say he covers; South takes the trick and the eight drops from West. Then once again he enters dummy and plays spades towards his hand. Now he has the A-6 of spades left over East's honour-5. The third finesse in the same suit is taken by playing the six when East follows with the five. Three finesses in the same suit! That's why this play was named Helgemo's triple finesse. What's next?

Geir Helgemo's partner in this game was, as mentioned, not just anybody. Edgar Kaplan was for many years editor of the world's most popular bridge magazine, *The Bridge World*. He was also a highly respected bridge player, analyst and theorist. The tournament Kaplan won with Geir Helgemo was his last victory. Before that he had had a series of outstanding results in many of the most prestigious tournaments around the world. But there was one title he never won. Many people regarded Kaplan as the best player in the world who had never won the Bermuda Bowl, the most prestigious tournament of them all. Let us hope it was not an omen that his last bridge victory came in the only event he ever played with Geir Helgemo. Several times since 1991 the Norwegian team, with Geir Helgemo on it, has been close to a triumph in the Bermuda Bowl. When this book was written Geir was still not 30 years old, so there are many reasons to hope that he will not inherit that special title from Edgar Kaplan.

Index